INSIDE THE LOCKER ROOM

True Stories From Dubuque's First National Champions

Denny Gibbons

D1521425

For my teammates,
for Jack & Kathy Barzee,
and for the great hockey fans of Dubuque.

Table of Contents

Foreword

This book is about a hockey a team that came together from many different walks of life to ultimately win a National Jr. A Hockey Championship, representing the City of Dubuque, Iowa. The stories are true to almost all the details, but I can only attest to the stories I knew about. I'm glad I didn't know about some of the others, it was better for the players, the team and the community. This book is filled with many different characters but it is also about the city of Dubuque, Iowa, its fans and a newly formed hockey organization called Mississippi Valley Inc. Together, they would experience an incredible eight-month journey that started in September of 1980 and would run through April 1981.

The author, Dennis Gibbons, whom I would coach from 1979-1982, was a sensitive young man. With a lot going on around him and with his teammates he was searching for answers. He was exceptionally hard on himself and suffered from a lack of confidence from time to time. I remember him telling me how much he looked up to his older brother Mike, and how he wanted to follow his footsteps in hockey and in life. I would come to understand him during this three-year period of time. In his quest to achieve his goals, he was driven and passionate about the path he would take. In the back of his mind his determination was not going to let him down. His moody and withdrawn personality was going to be a thing of the past. His last season playing for me he was a much happier individual. He was a true team player on and off the ice.

To me the city of Dubuque is a vibrant place with a distinct personality. It is a river town bordering Wisconsin and Illinois with rolling hills, charming neighborhoods and beautiful scenery. It is full of interesting history, old homes and buildings that give you inquisitive thoughts. There are old tunnels under the downtown with connections to Al Capone. The Majestic Five Flags Theater (The Orpheum Theatre) is part of the Five Flags Center that the Saints hockey team would call home.

One of Dubuque's magnificent views of the Mississippi, the Dubuque business district and the three states of Wisconsin, Illinois and Iowa, comes from Fenelon Place. The Fenelon Place elevator, the world's shortest and steepest railway, 296 feet in length starts on Fourth Street and elevates passengers 189 feet to the top. Julien Dubuque was a French-Canadian fur trader and the first settler to the area. He also has the bridge connecting Dubuque, Iowa to East Dubuque, Illinois named after him. Dubuque is the oldest city in Iowa.

The fans got a taste of what hockey was all about during the 1979-80 hockey season when the Waterloo Black Hawks played five of their home games at the Five Flags Center. The marriage between the fans, the youth hockey players and the parents for this exciting brand of hockey had begun. The attendance grew and there was a buzz on the streets for the new show in town.

As the fan base grew and the winning ways of the team progressed, the atmosphere became electrifying. Feeding off this energy, the players were pulled into a closely-knit team on a mission. Their achievements, sacrifices and life-long memories will be with them forever.

I hope that whoever reads this will enjoy it as much as I have enjoyed living it in real-time and again while reading this book. This was a huge part of my life. To the game of hockey, the players, the fans, the owners of the team, the youth hockey players, the parents and the great city of Dubuque, I THANK YOU.

- Jack Barzee

Preface

The stories you are about read are true events as told by the players of the 1980-81 Dubuque Fighting Saints Junior A hockey team and members of the Dubuque hockey community. Painstaking efforts were used to confirm each story with at least two sources and/or specific newspaper articles and/or other documentation. In writing some of the stories creative license was used to portray the actual events as documented and/or remembered by those taking part. The actual dates of the stories in the Regular Season chapter were closely matched to fit that point in the season but most likely did not happen on a specific day or week listed in the chapter heading.

Clearly some of the dialogue has been fabricated to enhance the stories, but some dialogue was taken directly from newspaper articles or notes that were kept from that time as well as the memories of those involved. Some of the dialog was created to replicate the personalities being portrayed by recreating their specific speaking methods and words. For example Worps consistently used the words "pathetic loser" throughout the season.

Most of the dates, Telegraph Herald newspaper headlines and other statistical information were gathered from the scrapbook created by Betty Weiland. Records on player careers and statistics were gathered from reliable Internet sources such as dubuquefightingsaints.com, ushl.com, eliteprospects.com and hockeydb.com.

It is important to realize that the context of these stories is set in a time when attitudes and laws were different. In 1980, the drinking age in Iowa was nineteen and the enforcement of intoxication laws was less stringent. People were regularly told by law enforcement to go directly home after being suspected of drinking and driving. Teenagers were not inundated with constant marketing ads to have a designated driver or face a jail sentence and a $10,000 fine, they were simply expected to be more responsible. The country was just starting to embrace the devastating effects of drinking and driving.

The stories in this book in no way reflect on the current Dubuque Fighting Saints organization except to represent the fans enthusiasm for the team and the game of hockey itself. The current Dubuque Fighting Saints franchise and the USHL are top-notch organizations focused on developing the premier hockey athletes in the country. They also put a heavy emphasis on building the character of those involved. There are strict rules in place that do not allow many of these types of stories from taking place today.

The fact that these stories happened in the early eighties does not excuse any or all of the actions in the pages ahead, but perhaps it gives you, the gentle reader, a frame of reference for the times they lived in and the choices they were making. After all, they were eighteen and nineteen year old males living far away from home for the first time in their lives.

Introduction

A 1982 Dubuque Fighting Saints Marketing Flyer read as follows:

"In May of 1980 a small group of hockey enthusiasts formed a corporation called Mississippi Valley Hockey Inc. They didn't know the team they would feature at the Five Flags Center in Dubuque, Iowa would turn into one of the most successful hockey stories in the country."

...This book is NOT that story!

You may have heard how the 1980-81 Dubuque Fighting Saints won 50 games in its first year, a league record. Or how they set attendance records many teams would envy today. Or how they won the scoring title, the goaltending title, the southern division title, the league title, the playoffs and the national championship. Less than twenty teenagers came to Dubuque from all around the country to play the game they loved. The coach, the community, the leaders, the volunteers, and the fans helped make their on-ice accomplishments a momentous success. This is all true but it is only part of the story.

The truly compelling stories come from inside the locker room, the bus rides, the bars, the houses, and in the community. Off the ice is where these players, the coach, and the people of Dubuque were unique. These are their true stories worth telling. Apparently the stories are worth telling over and over, time after time, because that is what these former players, now nearing 60 years old, have been doing for years when they get together.

These aren't the "glory days" stories old people tell because they have nothing to talk about, or the fishing tales that grow larger every year. These are true stories of ineptitude and failure, gross negligence and sheer luck, personality disorders and strange encounters. Some of them can't be printed...most are past the statute of limitations.

Prologue

December 1st, 2017

Mystique Community Ice Center, Dubuque, Iowa

The two female Saints fans were nervous. The game between the Dubuque Fighting Saints and the Rough Riders was in overtime. They were literally sitting on the edge of their seats as the puck moved around the boards in the defensive zone. A big Rough Rider defenseman got the puck near the blue line and fired a hard slapshot towards the net. The fan sitting on the left closed her eyes, waiting for the air to be let out of the arena.

Earlier in the third period, the Saints were down by a goal but were relentless in their attack. After several minutes of pressure they tied the game sending most of the fans into a joyous celebration, but not her. She had seen this before. "These are the type of games championship teams need to win," she thought. She couldn't handle another overtime disappointment.

This time the Saints goalie made a good save. He dropped to the ice deflecting the slapshot into the corner with his right pad. A Saints defenseman picked up the puck and passed it to a breaking winger cutting across the high slot. He received the pass in stride, moved it out of the zone, then passed it to a teammate cross ice. The Rough Riders were now on their heels, scurrying back to cover in their defensive zone.

The Saints controlled the puck for several long seconds before getting a shot in the high slot area. Two Saints placed themselves in front of the goalie, blocking his view. The Rough Rider goalie never saw the puck, but he got lucky. It deflected off his shoulder floating towards the corner. A Saints forward got to it just as hit the ice and skated it one stride towards the net. He forced a pass through the crease to a waiting teammate on the other side. The pass caught his teammate off guard. He hesitated for a fraction of a second before slapping at it twice, catching a piece of the puck on his second try. The puck dribbled into the net for the game-winning goal. It wasn't pretty but it counted.

The sixteen hundred and forty-two fans at the Mystique Community Ice Center jumped to their feet celebrating the victory for the Saints. Up in the owner's suite, Doctor David Field pumped his fist, "YES! They needed that," he said. Other notable fans among the joyous crowd were Richard Lehnhardt, Tom Harjehausen, and Nancy Scherr. These were some of the die-hard Saints fans back in 1980 that continue to support the Saints to this day.

Tom Hill, another die-hard Saints fan back in the eighties, was not in attendance. Tom could normally be seen standing with one foot on the railing cheering on his team, but the eighty-year-old gentleman with a pleasant smile and a quiet demeanor was not there. He was in western Iowa hunting with his boys.

As the two female Saints fans packed up their belongings to head home, the formerly nervous fan on the left confidently proclaimed, "These are the type of games championship teams win!"

Nickname Guide:

#1 Brian Granger	Granger
#2 Glen Gilbert	Bucky
#3 Michael Fallon	Fallon, Mike
#4 Curt Voegeli	Vogy
#5 Dennis Gibbons	Gibby
#6 Melvin Bailey	Battleship, Mel
#7 Christopher Guy	Guy, Chris
#8 Glenn Scanlan	Scanny
#9 Robert Motzko	Badger, Motz
#10 James Walsh	Walshy
#11 James Grillo	Gringo, Jimmy
#12 Jeffery Regan	Reegs
#16 Michael Carlson	Bulldog
#17 Brian Collins	Collins
#18 Jon Nordmark	Nordsy
#19 Tod Worpell	Worps
#20 Dean Thomas	Deano
#21 John DiNapoli	DiNap
#22 John Cook	Cookie
#30 Mark Jasken	Jask, Jasky
Coach Jack Barzee	Jackie-Boy, Silver Fox
Trainer Timothy Feldman	TD
Linesman Alan Stoltz	Stoltzy, Al
Linesman Michael Waddick	Waddy
Physician David Field	Doc, Doc Field

Chapter 1: Creation

November 6th, 1979

D riving the old Ford truck past Independence, Iowa the two middle aged fathers were traveling west on Highway 20 at 55 miles per hour on the two lane highway. They sat in silence for most of the drive. Two hours earlier they met at the Shot Tower restaurant in Dubuque to have a late lunch. The Shot Tower was one block south of the beautiful new civic center complex known as the Five Flags Center.

During lunch Doug asked Tom "Did you call Jack?" referring to Jack Barzee, the coach and owner of the Waterloo Black Hawks.

"Of course I did, you told me too," replied Tom as he took a bite of his hoagie sandwich.

Doug Jass and Tom Hill were fathers of boys that played in the newly formed Dubuque County Youth Hockey Association (DCYHA). In fact, they both helped to get the organization started. Their kids loved playing hockey and would spend whole days playing on the few frozen outdoor rinks and ponds Dubuque had during the winter. They agreed to leave the boys at home for this trip even though they both wanted to bring them with to see the game. They agreed earlier that this is business; there would be other occasions to bring the boys.

"What did he say? What was he like?" Doug wanted more information on Barzee.

"He said he'd talk to us after the game," Tom replied. "Just settle down will ya, I'd like to finish my sandwich."

After lunch they were going to see the Waterloo Black Hawks take on the Hennepin Nordiques in a United States Hockey League Junior A game at the old McElroy Auditorium in Waterloo. The McElroy was built in 1919 to house National Cattle Congress events. In 1962, they added the ice surface to be used during the winter by the Black Hawks. It seated 5100 people for a hockey game.

As they got closer to Waterloo, Doug started in again "Did it seem like he was interested?"

"I'm not sure, but he's willing to meet with us so, yah, I guess that means he is," said Tom.

"What are we going to say?" said Doug.

"We talked about this with the other guys," Tom replied referring to the guys on the DCYHA board when they met last week. "We don't have to reinvent the wheel. Waterloo has a good youth program, we'll find out what's working over there and copy it. Maybe he's willing to give us some other advice as well."

They got to the arena, paid the $4 each for their tickets and took their seats. "Looks like there's only a couple hundred people here, what do you estimate?" Tom asked.

"Oh, I think it's more than that, like 350, 400 maybe," said Doug. There were a lot of empty seats but it was a big place and the fans were spread out.

It was quiet in the arena as the game progressed. In the third period, a guy wearing number six for the Black Hawks, listed in the program as Mel Bailey, dropped his gloves and started fighting with a Hennepin player named Kurt Madryga. The sparse crowd came to life in a hurry. These two players were the premiere fighters in the league and did not disappoint. Toe-to-toe they went for more than a minute. The referees left them alone until they fell to the ice in a human ball, clutching and grabbing each other, exhausted and bloodied.

"Wow, pretty intense," said Doug.

"Pretty good hockey," replied Tom not really watching the fight. He was watching the bench, keeping an eye on the coach to get feel of what he would be like when they met later.

After the game, they were inside the coach's office as Jack Barzee was looking over the game statistics. After they exchanged pleasantries Jack said, "What can I do to help you guys?" Before they could answer, Jack returned to studying his stat sheets.

"Well, it's like I told you on the phone Mister Barzee. We need some advice on growing our youth program," Tom said. "We've got this brand-new hockey arena, but we are really struggling with fund raising and getting more kids involved."

Jack sat up at full attention now. "You didn't mention the arena on the phone. What's the story with that?" He asked.

They talked at length about the newly created Five Flags Center in Dubuque. Jack was keenly interested as Tom and Doug told him how it all happened. The Five Flags Arena was part of a project to restore the Majestic Theater, which was scheduled for demolition in 1972. Twice the city tried to pass a referendum to restore the old theater and twice it failed.

"We need to have an ice sheet in this referendum or it will fail again," Steve Peters director of the project stated publicly. The project committee finally added the arena as part of the referendum and it passed by a 4 to 1 margin.

"That's amazing! "Tell me more," said Jack wondering what kind of people would pass a bond referendum like that during a recession. Never mind that the country was not actually in a recession when it passed in 1974, Jack was creating a vision in his own mind.

Construction started in 1976 and the Five Flags Center, with multipurpose arena, was officially opened on March 24th of 1979. There was only one problem. They had no plan for what to put on the ice that would attract people to fill the 2642 seats. The seats remained empty for most of 1979, except for an occasional concert or Ice Capades show.

"What if the Black Hawks play some regular season games in Dubuque this year? Is 4 or 5 games enough?" said Jack. "We would need about 700 paid seats to make money. I would take a cut off that, the other team would get some travel and expense money, and then the rest would go into your youth program"

Tom and Doug were flabbergasted. That was way over their heads. "I don't know about that," said Tom as he paused to take it all in. "Give us a week or two to see what we can put together." Both Tom and Doug were thinking the same thing. They had just created a whole pile of work back in Dubuque and a whole pile more people needed to get involved...and they better get started!

"Oh, one more thing," Jack added as they were walking out. "I'll also need a two-thousand-dollar retainer to make it happen."

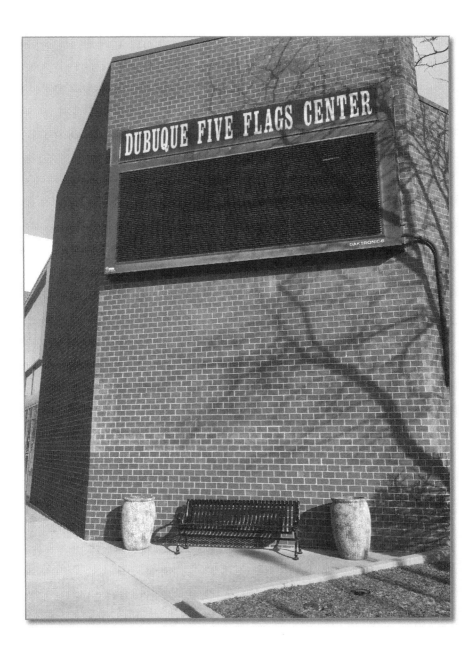

December 1979 and early 1980

There were many more people involved now. Frank O'Conner, Tim O'Brien, Jim Denman, Chuck Haas, Tom Trausch, Robert Kunnert, and Chuck Bailey all helped in addition to Tom and Doug. With this group, the required preparations were completed faster than they expected.

It was all set. The Waterloo Black Hawks would play 5 games in three months at the Five Flags Center. Jim Denman went to the bank and signed a note as the DCYHA treasurer that would guarantee the Black Hawks organization $2000 should the gate fees not cover the costs.

The first game in December drew 700 fans in attendance. The second, third and fourth drew an average of 900 and in the last game over 1100 people came into the Five Flags Center to watch Junior A hockey. Most of the fans didn't know much about hockey but they enjoyed the action. In fact, there were several occasions during the games when the puck would go out of play over the glass. The Dubuque fans would race to get the puck and immediately throw it back onto the ice. They had no concept of those pucks being souvenirs. The thought was that play could not continue if they didn't have the puck.

DCYHA had taken a big risk but it paid off. They never had to dip into the $2000 note to pay bills and the proceeds helped the youth association immensely. Interest in hockey spiked and the number of kids in the youth program doubled.

Now the question became "What do we do next year?" Jack Barzee had a plan for that. He made a series of phone calls and arranged a number of meetings in Dubuque in early 1980. He visited several times with interested people willing to invest in creating a new USHL franchise in Dubuque. Well, maybe not a totally new franchise.

Jack was in negotiations to buy the Hennepin Nordiques, bring them to Dubuque and sell his Black Hawks to local interests in Waterloo. It was a complicated deal and a lot of things had to fall into place to make it happen, but such was the mind of the 39-year-old Jack Barzee.

Jack was born in New Haven Connecticut. He started skating at age 4 and joined the competitive youth program at 6. He was always playing with, and against, older much larger players. What he lacked in size he made up for with speed and agility. In high school, he was playing with the only senior hockey team in New Haven.

After high school Jack tried out and made a Canadian Junior A team but had to leave when they did not allow Americans a visa to work in Canada, he simply couldn't afford to stay. He then tried out for the 1962 US National team (back then this was the USA Olympic team) making it through half the season before finally being cut in late January. From there he moved back and forth between senior teams and minor league pro teams until his arrival in Waterloo, Iowa to play for the Black Hawks at the start of the 1965 season. The USHL was a semiprofessional league at the time and the players got paid about $25-$50 per game.

Jack met Kathy Ellsworth after one of his games in March of 1967 and they were married in August of 1968. Kathy was born and raised in Waterloo, the third of four children. She was outgoing and talkative but also expressed a shyness and kindness that was refreshing. She enjoyed watching Jack play hockey and even liked the fights ...as long as they weren't cheap. Kathy spent many hours waiting for Jack after games because he was always the last one out of the locker room.

Jack continued to play for the Black Hawks until 1976 when he was forced, begrudgingly, into retirement at age thirty-six to become the coach. Being told you could no longer play the game was a difficult thing for Jack to accept. Coaching was a job he was ill prepared for but he soon figured out how to stay out of the way. It was a skill he developed as his coaching career progressed.

To complicate things, Jack and Kathy also adopted two boys, Zach in 1975, and Joel three years later. Things were difficult financially but Jack had no intention of leaving his first passion so he had to figure out a way to make coaching his career.

By 1979 Jack obtained ownership of the Waterloo Black Hawks but the organization was barely making ends meet. Now, in 1980, the Dubuque deal might help to solidify his financial situation and he could continue to coach...if all the pieces of the puzzle fell into place. Jack made it clear that he would not leave Waterloo unless he could sell the team locally. He also made it clear to the USHL board of directors that he wanted to retain the rights to his returning players from Waterloo and the new Waterloo owners would retain the rights of the Hennepin players. Jack was loyal beyond expectation.

Jack got what he wanted and when he finally secured a group of buyers for the Waterloo franchise the plan was set into action. On May 12th, 1980, an organization in Dubuque was formed called Mississippi Valley Hockey Inc. On May 20th, the USHL approved the deal and created a 48 game schedule for the Dubuque team, with 24 games to be played at the Five Flags Center.

The list of Mississippi Valley Hockey Inc. stock holders was long: Jack Barzee, Dr. David Field, Dr. Mike Nelson, Dick Michels, Dr. Dave Howell, Dr. Roger Ott, Dr. John Moberly, Dr. Anthony Piasecki, Dr. Robert Pfaff, George Beaves, Jim Kunnert, and Robert Kehl. Jim Houts came onboard later in 1980. This is the organization that created the Dubuque Fighting Saints, the Five

Flags Center now had a purpose and Jack Barzee now had a salary of $16,000 a year.

June 1980

For the Barzee family the move to Dubuque was very difficult. It helped that the boys were still young but there were other issues that took time to overcome. Kathy was having difficulties leaving her hometown and her close friends. Jack's new position as Coach and General Manager of the new Dubuque Fighting Saints required a lot of time and energy. The summer and early fall were the most challenging time in their marriage but they worked it out together. The early success of the Saints organization also helped alleviate some of the stress.

During that summer Jack had to take on all the tasks at once. With the Saints being a new organization in town everything had to be started from scratch. He had to sell season tickets, take out ads and create promotions in newspapers, billboards and radio, compose the game program and sell program ads. He had to order equipment: sticks, pucks, pads, gloves, breezers and jerseys. He had to line up hotels, meals and buses for the road trips. Then, at the same time, he needed to get new recruits and stay in touch with the returning players. If he couldn't put a competitive team on the ice all the other work would be in vain.

He also had a board of directors that he had to meet with on a regular basis to give status updates. He had to meet with league representatives and coordinate with the Five Flags Center personnel. In the community, he had speaking engagements with local groups and interviews with the media. He needed to keep the Saints in the public eye on a constant basis or he could lose the momentum built by last year's games and news of the new sport coming to Dubuque.

Jack needed help with housing players and organizing the initial training camp that could see as many as 40 players trying out over the course of a week. He enlisted the help of the DCYHA people who had been so helpful with the games played at the Five Flags Center the season before. Most of those folks were eager to help.

Finally, he needed to sell his house in Waterloo and complete the moving process. It was not humanly possible to get this all done by himself. The first person he hired was Betty Weiland as his secretary, but she would also be in charge of ticket sales, marketing and just about everything else that needed to be done. She had to take over a lot of Jack's duties so he could focus on the team when the season began.

Betty was one of the most gracious people Jack could have hired, but then again, Jack was finding out that most of the people in Dubuque were that way. There were two problems with hiring Betty; one was that the organization could only afford to pay for a part time position. (Authors note: compare this to the current Saints staff of 7 full-time office personnel, and several other part-time personnel that work from home or other parts of the country, in addition to a 3 person coaching staff). The second thing was that Betty knew absolutely nothing about the game of hockey.

"Here's a rule book," Jack said as he handed Betty the 600+ page AHAUS Hockey rule book that governs the teams in the USHL. "Read it over when you get a chance but don't worry about it too much, you'll do just fine."

Betty's office was under the seats at the Five Flags Center and it was always cold, even with a space heater. On game days Betty would leave early and come back a couple hours before the game to sell tickets at the front gate. Betty made a little over minimum wage but she also got four free tickets to home games for her kids.

"Jack was always so grateful for anything I did and he was the best boss I had in my entire working life," Betty said four decades later.

The next hire for Jack was Tim "TD" Feldman as the part time trainer for the team. TD was an emergency medical technician (EMT). His services would be needed on the bench for injuries during home games and as many away games that he could fit into his schedule. He would be the only other personnel Jack would have on the bench for most of the season. There was no money in the budget for an assistant coach.

TD was a fun loving curly haired young man that was not much older than the players he would be caring for. He lived hard and played hard because he potentially did not have much time to live. TD was born with a rare heart issue. He was initially not expected to live to adulthood without a transplant. He carried on with his life while waiting for a suitable donor to become available, but he never talked about it. He had every right to be bitter and self-loathing but he wasn't. He always had a smile and a unique laugh that the players heard often from the bench and in the locker room.

TD loved the game of hockey and played goalie for Kunnert's in the newly formed adult league. Like most goalies TD was little bit crazy. No one volunteers to step in front a net where people are shooting hard rubber pucks as fast as they can. TD was a trill seeker; he liked the idea of a puck hitting him in the head at 80 miles per hour.

"Have you guys been down to the 5 Flags yet to see Barzee?" TD said. He was talking to Al Stoltz and Mike Waddick, two of his Kunnert's teammates.

"Not yet," said Al. "You are so lucky man. That would be so cool to be part of the team. I can't wait for the season to start."

"I'd go talk to him soon if I were you. I think he's looking for some goal judges," TD said enthusiastically.

Later that week Al made an impromptu phone call to Mike "Get over to my house right now. Barzee is over at Doug Jass' house. Doug said he would introduce us to Jack," Mike hung up the phone, grabbed his keys and bolted out the door.

"Nice to meet you Mister Barzee," Al said with an awestruck smile on his face. "Mike and I would like to know if we can help out with the Saints somehow. Like, pick up pucks or something after practices, maybe move nets for you. You know, something for us to get a little ice time?"

"Doug tells me you guys are pretty good skaters," Jack replied. "You guys ever think about being linesmen?"

"Ah...sure, that would be great," Al said looking at Mike and hoping he was on the same page.

Mike said, "Jack, we would love to be officials but neither of us have ever refereed a hockey game. We might know what offside and icing is but, quite frankly, we don't have any training and we've never read a rulebook." While Al was willing to do anything, Mike was being realistic. He knew the USHL didn't just pull people off the street to be officials.

"Don't worry about training. They have a clinic in Madison in September. You guys study up on the rules and take a test. You'll be fine. I'll give you a phone number you can call to get registered. Here are some rulebooks," Jack said. Jack obtained a box of rulebooks from AHAUS to hand out to people in Dubuque. It was his way of educating people in the community on the game of hockey.

"This is kinda crazy, but it sounds like fun," Al said to Mike on the way home.

"Yah think?" Mike replied with sarcasm "This is beyond crazy! We better start reading this stupid rulebook!"

Al was naïve. He was just looking to be part of the new "show" in town. Mike, on the other hand, knew they were in over their heads. There was no training clinic or rulebook that would prepare them for what was in store. They would have to learn through experience...and what an experience it would be.

From the Desk of . . . **JACK BARZEE**

July 1, 1980

Dear Dennis,

I am inviting you to come to Dubuque the weekend of the 26th and 27th of July. This will give a small number of you players an inside track on the housing and job situation in Dubuque and a chance to see the town.

Let me know as soon as possible if you can make it. If you can't, it's not a big deal.

Yours truly,

J.B

The Number One coach
in the USHL!

P.S. How about some beer money!

**DUBUQUE FIGHTING SAINTS
UNITED STATES HOCKEY LEAGUE**

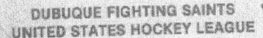

P.S.: Gibby owed Jack one month rent from the previous season.

Chapter 2: Arrivals

September 1980

They were all teenagers. They had to be, it was a prerequisite of the league. An eligible player must be a United States citizen under the age of twenty on October 1st. They came to Dubuque from all over the country. They came from places in the east like Vermont, Connecticut, New Jersey, New York and Illinois. They came from States out west like Colorado, Utah and Nevada. Some came from Wisconsin, but most came from Minnesota.

The first of the arrivals in Dubuque was Worps. Worps' real name is Tod Worpell, that's one "d" two "l "s. It is pronounced as "Todd Worp-ell." Most people mispronounced his name as Ted Worple. Gibby giggled every time they announced his name at the start of road games. "C'mon, it's not that hard of a name to read!" Worps said. One time he was announced as Ted Kopple (the ABC Nightly News anchor at the time). Worps didn't care after that, he accepted whatever they called him and shook his head.

Worps was from Las Vegas, Nevada. He was one of the veterans that Jack Barzee brought over from Waterloo along with Gibby, Cookie, Badger, Reegs, and Mel.

During the summer, after the season in Waterloo, Worps stayed in Minnesota with Gibby for several weeks, played some "pick up" games and worked odd jobs when he could. When the time to go back to Iowa drew near, Worps bought a car from one of Gibby's high school friends for $25. Like Worps, this car had issues. The main problem (for the car) was idling. If it came to a complete stop, as required by law, the engine would stall. Having to restart the engine in the middle of an intersection was precarious at best, so most of the time Worps would roll through stop signs and stop lights slowly. He got his first ticket in Preston, Minnesota near the Iowa border and another in Guttenburg before finally making it to 433 Bluff Street in Dubuque. This is the place that would house a majority of the players. (Author's Note: If you think it's distracting looking at a map on a smart phone while driving, try using a full size atlas like they did in the 80's.)

Barzee put him to work immediately collecting mattresses for all the players that would be arriving for tryout camp. For his efforts, Worps got to choose the best of the worst mattresses that the local housing authorities were throwing away.

Jeff Regan (Reegs) brought Mark Jasken (Jask) down from St. Cloud with him. Reegs drove his brown Ford Pinto and Jask followed in a U-Haul truck carrying all their belongings for the year. In Waterloo the year prior, Reegs was a key part of the Black Hawks success. Originally cut by the Hennepin Nordiques, he scored 33 goals in 48 games and helped the Black Hawks earn a spot in the national tournament.

Reegs was a fun loving forward that seemed to piss off opposing teams. One time he hit a St. Paul Vulcan player with a high stick and cut his face open. Reegs claimed it was an accident; he was trying to slash a different Vulcan player and missed. He was never penalized for the mishap. The guy left the rink to get stitches and returned later in the second period but stood next to the gate watching the game. When play moved to that end of the rink, the stitched player opened the gate and chased after Reegs at full speed. Reegs saw that he was coming at him and ducked. The stitched player fell over Reegs smashing his face on the ice, re-opening his original wound. He grabbed Reegs trying to scratch out his eyeballs but the linesmen pulled him off.

As the linesmen were taking the Vulcan player off the ice Reegs gave him a "bye-bye" wave with his gloved hand. This infuriated the Vulcan player so much so that he was able to get free of the linesmen and chased Reegs around the ice, leaving a trail of blood from his smashed face. Reegs was giggling and smiling at the guy while avoiding his grasp. The linesmen were chasing the Vulcan player and finally caught up with him before he could catch Reegs. The linesmen finally dragged the guy off the ice for good. It was quite a circus, but Reegs could do that to just about anyone ...if he wanted to. Ironically, that St. Paul Vulcan moved to Dubuque to play for the Saints the following year.

Reegs was five-feet ten inches and weighed 170 pounds. At age 19 he was already suffering from a receding hairline but could grow lots of hair everywhere else. Barzee had informed him that he would be one of the captains of the Saints along with Mel Bailey. To keep it from being a popularity contest, coach Barzee selected the captains based on leadership skills but most of the players thought it was based on baldness.

During the summer Reegs enticed his St Cloud Apollo High School goalie (Jask) to come down to Dubuque with him to play for the Saints. When Jask heard of the opportunity he was all-in. He had no real plans after graduating from high school so this sounded like a dream come true, but he would have to make the team first.

Jask was short for a goalie at five-foot eight. He was skinny at 165 pounds but he was in the best shape of his life. He was the type of guy that loved to interact with people. To Jask, his teammates were his best friends. He was personable and listened intently whenever a teammate was speaking. Jask had some struggles in hockey his senior year in high school and had a little bit of an independent streak. Reegs wondered if Coach Barzee and Jask would mesh.

They travelled from St. Cloud to Austin, Minnesota to pick up Badger. Then they traveled as a group to the house on Bluff Street where Worps was waiting for them. Worps gave Badger and Reegs a big hug. "I missed you guys so much ...especially this shiny part," he said to Reegs as he rubbed the top of his head.

A couple days later John Cook (Cookie) drove into town and parked his silver Nova at the house on Bluff Street. As a veteran Cookie was sure to make the team, so he picked out a quiet room on the top floor and moved in all his belongings.

Cookie was a six-foot 200-pound hulk of a forward from Bountiful, Utah. In fact, his body resembled the real Hulk from the comic book, minus the green skin. He had a handsome face with thick sandy brown hair. Cookie was quiet and reserved. Though he rarely got into fights, on the ice he played tough and could shoot and pass the puck as well as anyone on the team. The year before, Cookie scored the game-winning, series-winning, goal that propelled Barzee's Black Hawks into the national tournament.

Mel Bailey drove his black Datsun 280Z into town on the same day and unloaded his stuff into the house on Bluff Street. Mel was not much of a social butterfly. He kept to himself and rarely added to conversations when the guys were talking.

Jim Walsh (Walshy) was a five-foot nine-inch, 155-pound forward that played high school hockey with Worps and Mel in Rosemount, Minnesota. In 1979 all three of them wanted to play hockey in the USHL. When Worps and Mel went to Waterloo, Walshy decided to stay in the Twin Cities because he had a good job. He tried out for the Hennepin Nordiques and played with them all season.

When the Hennepin player's rights were transferred to Waterloo in 1980, Walshy wanted to rejoin his high school teammates in Dubuque so Jack acquired his rights. Surprisingly, Waterloo released Walshy during the summer without requiring a trade. Walshy came down to Dubuque and eventually moved into the 11th Street apartments, where several other players were staying.

About the same time as Mel, Jimmy Grillo came into town with his parents. They helped move him into the house on Bluff Street. Jimmy's cousin, Billy Grillo, was Barzee's best player in Waterloo the year before. Billy asked Jack to come up to Hibbing, Minnesota, during the summer to entice Jimmy to come play in Dubuque. Born and raised on outdoor rinks in Hibbing, Jimmy Grillo was a solidly built five-foot ten-inch forward and was a strong skater.

Mike Fallon and Jon Nordmark were the only two high school aged kids on the tryout list. Jack made arrangements for Jon to stay at the Doug Jass house and Mike with the Jim Denman family during try-outs. If they made the team they would live there for the rest of the season. Jon flew in from Colorado and was picked up at the airport by Doug. Mike drove his old Chevy truck all the way from New York by himself. When he crossed the border into Iowa, he was supposed to call Jim Denman to let him know he arrived in Dubuque. He never made the call.

Mike Fallon was from Farmingdale on Long Island. He was looking for the opportunity to play hockey at a more competitive level than what was being offered out east. At six-foot one, 180 pounds, he was bigger and better than most players in his age group in New York. He also had a full mustache and could grow a thick beard in three days if he didn't shave.

It was the first time he set foot in Iowa and Mike was unsure what he wanted to do next. He knew he was supposed call Jim Denman but he procrastinated. He drove to the outskirts of town and saw some cows feeding

34

near a fence. He pulled over, got out and watched the cows picking at the grass from up close. He had never seen real cows before. After a several minutes, he got back in the truck and continued to the Five Flags Center. Mike roamed the arena for an hour then checked into the nearby Julien Dubuque Hotel for the night. He would call Jim Denman tomorrow, after the first tryout session, if he thought he had a real chance of making the team.

Glen Gilbert (Bucky) and Curt Voegeli (Vogy) were two of a kind from the east coast. They both were recommended to Jack Barzee by their high school coaches. Bucky was from Northfield, Vermont, Vogy was from Cheshire, Connecticut.

They were both approximately six-foot 200-pound defensemen. They flew in on the same day and arrived at the Julien Dubuque hotel where they would stay until after they made the team. Bucky was gregarious and loud but still somehow made friends quickly. He did not seem to lack self-confidence but was also compassionate and humble. Vogy was more quiet and introspective. He lacked self-confidence but shouldn't have; his skills were as solid as his muscular build.

"Vogy was always harder on himself than I could have ever been," Barzee said.

"I always thought Jack didn't like me," Vogy said.

Barzee would have to handle each of these characters differently, but that was Jack's special skill.

After getting released by Green Bay, Barzee picked up Chris Guys' rights almost immediately. At 155 pounds it was theorized that Guy would get pushed around, or broken in half, but Barzee knew that Guy did magical things with the puck and was a solid enough skater. Jack thought that Guy was able to see the ice well enough to keep himself out of trouble. Chris Guy made it into Dubuque before tryouts and moved into the upper floor on Bluff Street as Reegs roommate.

Mike "Bulldog" Carlson drove down from northern Minnesota in his blue 1974 Dodge Dart. His intention was to park his car at the house on Bluff Street and only use it to go home for Christmas and then finally to get home at the end of the season. For the most part, that is what happened.

The Bulldog nickname was misleading. Carlson was not a rough, tough, stocky forward like a real bulldog. He was quite the opposite. Bulldog was not muscular, and was small at five-feet eight inches. He was not overweight, but he still had a little baby fat around the midsection. Even with that build, he had a strange knack for scoring goals. He scored from everywhere on the ice, and he scored in bunches. Some said he was just lucky, but nobody could be that lucky. Barzee knew that his skill was not something he could coach into other players. It was just something Bulldog had. Bulldog would use it, and use it a lot. Carlson got the name Bulldog because everyone thought that he would be playing for the University of Minnesota Duluth...the Bulldogs. He grew up and played high school hockey in the small town of Two Harbors, Minnesota, just a stone's throw north of Duluth. Worps sarcastically referred to Two Harbors as "Couple Swamps."

As Dean Thomas (Deano) and Brian Collins drove through Rockford, Illinois, on their way to Dubuque they shared stories of their young hockey playing days in the Park Ridge suburb of Chicago. Deano played goalie for the squirt team when they won the Illinois state championship. The next year Deano wanted to score goals with his buddy Brian so he became a forward. These two played their youth hockey together all the way through to their high school club team.

In the 70's hockey in the Chicago area was very unorganized. Illinois schools did not have sanctioned teams, so a student could play for any organization in addition to their high school club team. Deano and Collins played together on the high school club team but Deano also played for one of the Triple A sponsored teams that travelled all over the country. Additionally, Collins played for the Chicago Minor Hawks, a local team that played against Chicago area college club teams.

After high school Deano went to Miami of Ohio, which was transitioning from a club organization to a full-fledged Division I college program. In the fall of 1980 Deano's dad got him the try out in Dubuque. Deano's dad also called Brian Collins and told him about the opportunity in Dubuque. Brian wasn't really sure what he wanted to do with his life but after talking to his old friend Deano, he decided to give Dubuque a try.

The two friends crossed over the bridge from East Dubuque, Illinois, and headed to the arena. They dropped their hockey equipment in the spare locker room and were given a room at the Julien Dubuque hotel.

Jack looked over the two six-foot, 180 pound Chicago natives as they entered the arena. "These guys are pretty big. I hope they can skate," he thought to himself.

"Tomorrow we start two-a-day tryouts so you two should probably get some rest," Jack advised. Deano and Collins dropped their bags in their hotel room...then went to the bar.

Denny Gibbons (Gibby) was finally heading back to Iowa to play hockey. He was looking forward to this for weeks if not months. At age 18 he was still considered young in his second year in the league. He was finally starting to feel confident in his game over the summer. He had come a long way from barely making the Waterloo team the year before.

It wasn't his skill that earned him a spot on the team. There were two Minnesota high school state champion players from Bloomington Jefferson that left the team early because they didn't have the stomach to "rough it up."

Gibbons didn't make his high school team in White Bear Lake, Minnesota...but he was willing to fight. However, just because he was willing didn't mean he was particularly good at it.

The program said he was five-foot eight and a half inches. All athletes lie about their height in the program. It's universal in all sports and well known. He was five-foot seven. At 180 pounds, he was short and stocky. Some said he was pudgy but most of his weight was carried in his thighs, which gave him balance on the ice. He was barely good enough to make a bottom dwelling North St Paul Junior B team after getting cut his senior year in high school. The St. Paul Vulcans had no interest in him so he petitioned his older brother Mike to get him a try out in Waterloo. Mike had a connection to Jack Barzee.

Gibbons brother gave him some advice as he left for Waterloo. "You have to prove to Barzee that you're tough. In practice, pick out someone your size and drop the gloves. Make sure you get the first punch in," he said. After several days of tryouts, the opportunity finally arose. A player named Murphy "lifted his cup." (Author's note: Cup lifting is when a player uses his stick to...uh, I think you get the picture.) Off came the gloves. Gibbons got the first punch in and clearly got the best of Murphy with multiple blows to his face. Murphy got in one punch towards the end of the fight that left a knot on Gibbons forehead. After practice, the knot was swelling grotesquely.

Coach Barzee called Gibbons into his office and sat him down to explain the situation. He said, "Gibby, you're gonna make the team," Gibbons let out a sigh as Barzee continued "...but you have to pick on someone tougher than Murphy!" Gibbons immediately covered his forehead with his hand in an attempt to hide the huge red knot that Murphy gave him. "Thanks Coach, I will."

The drive from the Cities was a beautiful one, especially along the Mississippi River. Gibbons was driving his big red Mercury Marquis. It was a "Boat" of a car and seated nine comfortably. On this trip it was filled with stuff, lots of stuff. He even had a refrigerator, with a beer tapper, strategically packed in the back seat so it wouldn't get damaged. He had no second thoughts about making the team this year so the car was full, so full that an 18-wheeler loaded with pigs passed him going up the long steep hill on the way out of Guttenburg.

The last part of the drive along the top of the hills through Rickardsville was particularly awesome. On each side of the road he witnessed elegant farms and beautiful houses up and down the bluffs for miles on both sides of the road, as far as the eye could see. It was truly breathtaking scenery on that September day and still is today. Shortly after Rickardsville the road slopes steeply downhill, twisting and turning near a small town called Durango. The road flattens out at Sageville then turns straight south for four miles to the outskirts of Dubuque.

He made his way to the house on Bluff Street. He would spend the next several months living in that house rooming with Worps and several others. Returning veterans Badger, Worps, Reegs, Mel, Cookie and newcomers Bulldog, Grillo, Jask, and Guy.

As a general rule, hockey players have nicknames that end in -ie or -y. Jim Walsh became Walshy, John Cook was Cookie, and Denny Gibbons was Gibby. However, this team had a lot of nicknames that deviated from the rule and some had no nickname at all. Mike Carlson's nickname was Bulldog. Bob Motzko's nickname was Badger, which was given to him by Worps. Grillo's cousin was Worps's High School hockey coach in Rosemount, Minnesota. He went by the nickname Gringo. In fact, all the males in the Grillo clan went by Gringo. Just like all the Cook's were Cookie's, all the Gibbons' were Gibby's, and all the Worps's...well, Worps was an original. Worps had brothers and sisters but there was only one Worps. Thank God for that! Melvin Bailey had a nickname of course, "Battleship Bailey," but it was too long. They just called him Mel.

The goal was to spend the rest of the day unpacking and getting settled in. Training camp and two-a-day practices didn't start until tomorrow so they had plenty of time.

The veterans were sitting in the living room relaxing and starting to nod off when the front door slammed open. Bulldog and Grillo ran in screaming, heading to the back of the house as fast as their feet could move. Startled from his catnap Gibby jumped to the edge of his seat "What the heck was that about?" he said.

Worps and Badger, who had been in Dubuque for several days, looked at each other from their relaxed positions on the couch and in unison said, "Pig truck." Apparently, the guys from northern Minnesota had never smelled a pig truck before. Pig trucks traveled down Bluff Street quite often but those northerners never got used to the smell.

Bob Motzko (Badger) had come down a week early with Reegs and Jasken to get to know the people and the places. Rumor had it he already had a girlfriend...or two. Badger was a handsome young gentleman and the ladies were attracted to him in droves. He was 5 feet 11 inches tall (program height) and 175 pounds of romance. Badger was also a social butterfly, a 1980's version of Facebook in the flesh, minus all the politics. He made friends everywhere, old and young alike, and probably could have run for office by the time he left Dubuque.

Originally from Austin, Minnesota, Badger started out the previous year playing for his hometown Austin Mavericks before moving to Waterloo to play for Barzee. In high school, they called him Breakaway Bob because he scored most of his goals on breakaways, but that was before Worps changed it to Badger.

After recovering from the pig truck scare, Grillo came down the stairs with a football. It was "game on!" right there in the house. Gibby was a natural center.

He hiked the ball to Badger. Badger would throw the ball way down field to Worps in the end zone. That was the plan anyway. Jasken and Grillo put the rush on Badger but they had to get through Gibby first. Guy tried to defend but Worps cut right at the TV and got a step on him. Carlson and Cookie sat in the end zone giggling like schoolgirls as Worps made a diving catch, landing right on top of them. Touch Down!

The "end zone" was actually a couch that was placed in front of the big bay window facing the street. That window pretty much covered the whole wall on that side of the house. And "way down field" was only 30 feet from the stairs. The place had a high ceiling so there was plenty of room for the long throw. It's a good thing Worps was sure handed or that window would have been...well, that would have been a fitting start to a season of mishaps and misadventures but it didn't happen. Somehow that window made it through the whole season.

"These rookies might fit in good," Gibby told Worps.

"Not so sure...they obviously suck at football," Worps replied loud enough for all to hear. That's Worps; he never missed an opportunity to impress.

"That was too close!" thought Badger "If Barzee saw this he'd be pissed." It was just like Badger. He was always the responsible one. Mature well beyond any of those present. "Hey, let's go play at Loras College," he said, averting a potential early season disaster.

"Wait, what's a Lor-ass College?" Jask asked.

Badger shook his head, "Let's go rookie." None of the others knew what or where Loras College was but it didn't matter. They were young athletes and it was time for a little football competition on some real green grass. They loaded up in Gibby's red "Boat" and headed to the college. (Author's note: Worps told Badger at the first reunion, "That was the closest I ever got to a college library.")

41

Inside The Locker Room

Soon the indoor football field on Bluff Street would be covered with the nasty mattresses Worps acquired for the three-day training camp. Many more prospects arrived for tryouts, 32 in all. Not all of them stayed on the football field. Barzee arranged for several of them to stay at the Julien Dubuque Hotel just a few blocks away, and some stayed with volunteer families in the community. Most were gone after the first couple days. Only a few remained to play in the preseason games.

The house on Bluff Street as it stands today. It now hosts psychic readings.

The Preseason Roster:

No Name	Pos	Height	Weight	Home Town
#1 Steve Glickman	G	6'	185	Skokie, IL
#2 Glen Gilbert	D	6'1"	180	Northfield, VT
#3 Mike Fallon	D	6'1"	180	Farmingdale, NY
#4 Curt Voegeli	D	6'	185	Cheshire, CT
#5 Denny Gibbons	D	5'8$^{1/2}$"	180	White Bear Lake, MN
#6 Mel Bailey	D	6'	190	Rosemount, MN
#7 Chris Guy	D	5'11"	155	Littleton, CO
#9 Bob Motzko	F	5'11"	175	Austin, MN
#10 Jim Walsh	F	5'9"	155	Rosemount, MN
#11 Jim Grillo	F	5'10"	170	Hibbing, MN
#12 Jeff Regan	F	5'10"	170	St. Cloud, MN
#14 John Lex	F	6'	200	Madison, WI
#16 Mike Carlson	F	5'9"	160	Two Harbors, MN
#17 Brian Collins	F	6'1"	175	Palentine, IL
#18 Jon Nordmark	F	5'9"	170	Westminster, CO
#19 Tod Worpell	F	5'10"	170	Las Vegas, NV
#20 Dean Thomas	F	6'	182	Park Ridge, IL
#21 Andy Fielding	F	5'10"	170	Glen Rock, NJ
#22 John Cook	F	6'	200	Bountiful, UT
#30 Mark Jasken	G	5'8"	165	St. Cloud, MN

Chapter 3: Preseason

October 4ᵗʰ, 5ᵗʰ & 6ᵗʰ, 1980:

Saints 5, Elmhurst Huskies 5 (away)

Saints 13, Elmhurst Huskies 7 (home)

Saints 8, Des Moines 5 (away)

"Fighting Saints justify name before 2400 fans" -Telegraph Herald

The roster was set...or so they thought. Although he never showed it outwardly Barzee was very skeptical about this group of players. Most of these players were cut from other teams, rejects from other leagues or simply had no other place to play.

Carlson was traded for a bag of pucks from St. Paul because they thought he was too small to play in the league. Chris Guy was released by Green Bay for the same reason. Fallon and Nordsy were standout high school players in their respective towns but opportunities there were limited, they were young and the only prospects still in high school. Jasken's decision to try out in Dubuque was at Reegs' urging, and mainly because he had nothing better to do at the time.

Grillo, Vogy and Bucky were recommendations from colleagues of Barzee, so he had no idea how they would turn out. Deano left the University of Miami (Ohio) after being cut.

Even the veterans were rejects: Badger was released from Austin, Reegs from Hennepin, Waterloo had Walshy's rights but let him go to Dubuque. Gibby was not even considered by any team because he was cut in high school. Cookie had no place to play in Utah. The Bloomington Jr. Stars cut both Mel and Worps the year before. There were many occasions when Barzee regretted his decision to keep Worps. Worps would haunt Barzee for two more years.

Barzee debated at length about cutting both Deano and Collins after training camp but decided to give them an opportunity in the preseason games. In fact, Deano, Collins, Bucky and Fallon spent the entire training camp in what the players referred to as the "Cut Locker Room." With 32 players trying out, Barzee had to separate the players into two locker rooms for the two-a-day tryout sessions. After each session, there would be two or three fewer players in the "Cut Locker Room." The next day would bring another couple players missing, and so on. After the third and final day of tryouts, only those four remained in the "Cut Locker Room."

"Lot's a room in here now, Jackie boy, do we have to move into the other room?" asked Bucky jokingly when Barzee entered the Cut Locker Room after the final tryout session.

"Not yet," said Barzee. "You guys have to earn your way onto the team in the exhibition games." Bucky's smile vanished.

Bucky and Fallon were defensemen. Barzee had already made his mind up about them. They had made the team, but he couldn't tell them that just yet. It was only Deano and Collins that he was unsure about. As always, Collins didn't say a thing, he just grinned and accepted the challenge.

This ragtag bunch of juveniles were about to embark on a storybook season, but something was needed to bring them together as a team. The Elmhurst Huskies, a team from Illinois that the Saints would play in two pivotal preseason games, would be the catalyst.

The first game was played in Elmhurst at the Polar Dome Ice Rink next to Santa's Village in Park Ridge, Illinois, Deano's hometown. The Huskies were a Junior A team just like the Saints, but they were in the Chicago Junior A League. That league had a requirement that all players must wear facemasks.

Facemasks were fairly new in late 1970's and they were preventing a lot of face injuries, specifically permanent eye injuries. Consequently, most state youth organizations and colleges were requiring them. They were not required in the USHL and the only Saints player to wear a facemask was Nordsy. He didn't start wearing it until after the Christmas break. The Bloomington Jr. Stars were the only USHL team that required facemasks during the 1980-81 season. The Saints thought they were "chicken-shit."

At some point during the season, rumors circled of facemasks being required by the Saints management. Worps was having none of that. He first protested to Barzee. When Barzee let it slip that Doc Field was the instigator, Worps went directly to Doc Field.

"When you get to college, you will have to wear one," was Doc Field's response.

"I'm not going to college, and I will never hide behind a facemask! If you make this rule, I guarantee you that half the team will request to be traded," replied Worps.

Ahhh, the old trade request ploy. Whenever a player felt they were getting screwed they would threaten to request to be traded. This only worked on successful teams and only by certain players. This was a risky move by Worps. At that point in his career, Worps was stretching his luck, not to mention stretching the truth about his teammates resolve on facemasks. Regardless, the ploy worked and the facemask rumors never resurfaced until the following season.

As soon as the Huskies skated onto the ice, the Saints players saw that the "enemy" was wearing facemasks. They knew this would get interesting.

"Don't lead with your chin, Mel. I'd hate to see you lose that pretty smile," Worps said. Mel had several scars from past fist and stick battles, and Mel rarely smiled. He had one long scar right below his mouth, which was delivered from a cross check to the chin in the previous season. This wasn't the first time Worps would antagonize Mel. Worps would do it constantly, all season long.

The game was rough and cheap. Barzee reminded everyone that they needed to skate hard and play hockey to make this team. "Ignore the cheap stuff," he said. They stayed disciplined and left Illinois with a tie but also a thirst for physical revenge in the next game a day later.

On October 5th they would be playing the same team in the first ever Dubuque Fighting Saints preseason home game. A packed house of over 2400 potential fans were eager to see what this new team, and this new sport, would look like...or what their own hockey team in Dubuque would look like. It would not be what many expected.

Most expected to see a hockey game; but what they got was a penalty fest, interrupted by numerous goals. Despite the best efforts of the referee, who was obviously informed about the rough play in the previous match, penalties didn't stop the Huskies from being cheap. And despite Coach Barzee's best efforts the Saints were retaliating.

"These guys aren't kids anymore, they're men now and I expect them to behave like men out there. But they can only be expected to take so much, after that, I can't do anything," said Barzee.

Some fights occurred but most were just pushing, shoving and wrestling. Mel punched a few facemasks but they did not fight back so Mel just ended up going to the penalty box for long periods of rest. The Huskies used their sticks (not to pass the puck) a little too often and the Saints responded with gloved fists to the facemasks. However, Deano was able to get a guy's mask off during a fight and give him a beating that required ten stitches, four of them on Deano's hand.

With less than three minutes to play, the game reached a crescendo. Cookie was carrying the puck into the attacking zone while holding off a Huskie defender. The defender hit Cookie across the head with his stick and kicked his skates out at the same time. It was the cheapest of cheap shots. Cookie flipped and landed on his head.

Before Cookie slid to a stop along the boards Barzee flamed out. "Somebody go get that son of a bitch!" Barzee screamed, almost jumping onto the ice himself. His attitude instantly changed to revenge and he released any restraints on the players...not that he could have stopped them in the first place.

Sensing Barzee's frustration and intensity, Gibby and Fallon, who were nearest to Barzee on the bench, jumped over the boards to take revenge. There was a melee along the boards where Cookie continued to lay motionless. Several players with facemasks were getting punched and some were even fighting back. Mel had one of the player's mask off and was beating him senseless. Linesmen Al Stoltz and Mike Waddick failed to hold Mel back. Finally, Mel told Stoltz he was finished. Stoltz then turned away to tend to the pulverized Elmhurst Husky player. Mel took advantage of this and got one more solid punch in on the guy for good measure.

After leaving the bench Fallon grabbed the closest player and threw him to the ice, gloves still on, punching furiously. Gibby went directly to a player that was trying to escape the melee towards the Huskies bench. That Huskie went into the turtle shell; a term used to describe a player that curls up in the fetal position to protect the face/head area. Gloves off and ready for revenge, Gibby grabbed the enemy facemask through the turtle shell cover and lifted it violently trying to get punches underneath and into his face. When this proved fruitless, as evidenced by his bloodied hand that caught part of the mask, he grabbed the Huskie players head with both hands and began pounding it on the ice until a linesman pulled him off.

Most of the fighting was going on in bunches over in the corner, away from the players' benches. The referee and linesmen were all focused in that direction so Gibby and Fallon thought they might get away with leaving the bench during the fight. That infraction will cost you a game misconduct, and you will be out for the next game as well.

Four players from each team were ejected. Gibby and Fallon got 2-minute penalties for roughing instead of game misconducts. That was a lucky break.

At the Five Flags Center, the penalty box sits adjacent to the player's bench and coach Barzee was pacing. As he rounded the bench near the penalty box, Gibby said, "How'd we do coach?" with a proud grin on his face. He nodded to Fallon standing next to him confident that they had extracted the revenge their coach requested.

"Pretty good, but you got the wrong guy!" Barzee barked at them. He was still pissed and it showed on his face. Gibby and Fallon moved to the far side of the penalty box to avoid any further interaction with Barzee.

Cookie lay on the ice after the fights were cleared up and a stretcher was brought out. As he was taken off the ice, he remained motionless. He spent the night in the hospital for observation and eventually got the all clear after two days. Cookie played in a couple more games but the guys could tell his heart was no longer in it. Sadly, despite Barzee's pleading, Cookie packed up his things, shoved them into his car and headed back to Utah never to play competitive hockey again.

The Saints won the game against the Elmhurst Huskies 13-7, but it proved to be costly in many ways. They lost Cookie, a good friend of the veterans as well as the newcomers. He was a talented player and a great personality that would have contributed greatly to the season.

John Lex was an extremely talented forward from Madison, Wisconsin. He scored multiple goals in his few games with the Saints, but he got homesick when his brother was an early cut and he also had enough of this type of hockey. He left the team soon after that game. Steve Glickman, a goalie from Skokie, Illinois, was also homesick and was released after playing in a few more games. Andy Fielding from New Jersey was also released.

Homesickness was a problem for a lot of these teenagers. Being away from home for the first time caused a lot of talented players to quit and go home. Barzee referred to them as "Home-Boys." Social media at that time was watching MTV or ESPN on this new invention called Cable TV. It would be another decade before Al Gore would create the Internet. They didn't have smart phones back then and they couldn't email. Communications to mommy consisted of writing home on actual paper and putting a postage stamp on an envelope or making a long-distance phone call from a pay phone. To call home they either called "Collect" or lined up dimes and quarters to get through the call without getting cut off. These guys couldn't afford telephones or cable TV in their apartments. (Author's note: For you young folks out there, "Collect" is when an operator asks the person on the receiving end to accept the charges for a long-distance call. Yes, there was an "operator" back then, and you had to pay extra for long-distance phone calls. Look it up on your smart phone!)

For the most part though, the players considered it a personal challenge to be on their own for the first time in their lives and loved the freedom it gave them. Doing your own laundry, buying/cooking your own food and paying rent was a responsibility of being an adult and although they didn't enjoy all of it, they accepted it.

One positive event occurred as a result of the Elmhurst game. Jack became convinced that Deano and Collins would be a good addition to the team. Deano proved he was scrappy and tough, he threw around Huskie players like rag dolls. Collins scored two goals, one while shorthanded, and assisted on three others, showing that the rough stuff never took him off his game. "I might have to put them on the same line...maybe Deano can protect Bulldog at center," Jack thought.

About half of the huge crowd that night was not excited about the style of play or the fighting. The other half loved it, just like they love watching Pro Wrestling. The fighting was a necessary sideshow in the game, but it was not the way the Saints would play in the future. They would fight when they had to. In fact, most of the players will record fighting penalties at some point during the season, but for the most part they would intimidate opposing teams by filling their nets with pucks. Mel would continue to be the tough guy, the enforcer for the team, and he would satisfy the Pro Wrestling crowd. It took several games and lots of wins to bring back that half of the crowd that was put out by the preseason fiasco. Some fans never returned.

The new Dubuque Fighting Saints played one more preseason game in Des Moines, which they won handily.

The Elmhurst fiasco brought the players together as one team. There were no longer any rookies. They were all veterans now, and they would be the core of the team that would give Dubuque its first Junior A national championship...if they didn't do anything stupid. "Fat chance of that," thought Barzee.

At home Jack told Kathy "If I can just keep them healthy...and out of jail, we might just have a chance with this crew." It was more pleading than confidence.

"They're nice boys," she replied. She knew the holdovers from Waterloo pretty well but had yet to meet most of the others. "It'll all work out honey. Don't let it bother you."

Jack had done everything off the ice that needed to be done to this point. He had more support from the community than he ever imagined. All the personnel were in place, all the other pieces of this organizational puzzle fit together in perfect order, and he had a huge crowd for the first home game...but to him, the team didn't look very good. He also had serious doubts about managing all the different player personalities.

"Well, we're in for a hell of ride," Jack said more to himself than to Kathy as he turned off the light. He knew this would be another restless night.

Chapter 4: Regular Season

October 9th, 1980:

Denman Family Home

"Fighting Saints play at St. Paul to open season" -*Telegraph Herald*

n his hand was a box of spaghetti. He studied it carefully and felt the weight thinking it would not be enough. He looked at the grocery list again and instantly came to a conclusion.

Jim hesitated with this decision only because he was already in the doghouse. Earlier in the day he called his wife Ginny and told her that he had invited the new hockey team over for supper.

"The whole team?" she screamed into the phone. "Tonight?" she added before he could answer the first question.

"Well, yes...and TD too, so I think we should plan on about 20 or so," Jim said.

"We don't have enough food here to feed that many," she replied still in disbelief.

"We just have to cook a bunch of spaghetti and butter some bread. Make a list of what we need. I'll stop by the Save-U-More on the way home." Jim replied. He used the term "We" implying that he would help with the cooking when Ginny knew he would be doing the entertaining and she would be doing most of the cooking.

Jim and Ginny Denman were another middle-aged Dubuque couple involved with the Dubuque Fighting Saints program. Besides trying to be good parents to their two boys, Tony 15, and Nathan 8, they saw the Saints as a way to help their business grow. Well, Jim did anyway. To Ginny it was just another one of his "involvements" that may or may not work out so well. He had a lot of those. Most turned out ok, some didn't.

Jim owned Oakridge Sports, a sporting goods store located to the west of the Kennedy Mall. When they opened the store in 1974, there was hardly any hockey equipment for sale. Tom Hill, Doug Jass and few others would go in there regularly and ask for sticks, pucks and other things to keep their kids supplied. Mike Waddick, Al Stoltz and the guys that played outside at Flora Park also needed equipment on occasion. A couple years back Jim got involved in the youth program and saw the potential for the hockey market in Dubuque. Last year, after the Waterloo Black Hawks played 5 games at the Five Flags Center, demand for hockey equipment in Dubuque skyrocketed, and now he had a whole section of his store devoted to hockey.

To Jim, feeding these guys before their first road trip seemed like the right thing to do. He knew they wouldn't eat very well on their own. "They probably haven't had a healthy meal since they got here," he presumed correctly.

"He can't just do a little here and little there, he has to go all in...on everything!" Ginny thought. "Oh well, for better or worse, I guess."

Back at the Save-U-More, Jim's decision was made. He would double the quantity of everything on Ginny's list. That should be adequate to feed 20 young men, plus TD...if he was lucky, Ginny wouldn't notice.

"We're going to be eating spaghetti for months," Ginny said as she started cooking, obviously aware that Jim tried to pull a fast one. Jim said nothing as he opened more boxes of spaghetti and added them to the large pot of boiling water.

Her comment passed without a response, mainly because he knew she didn't want to hear one. "You have no idea how much 18-year-old athletes can eat," he thought to himself but was smart enough not to say it out loud.

The players started rolling in around 5:30. Fallon lived with the Denman's, so he was helping out by opening the front door and giving instructions on where to put the coats. Fallon was one of the lucky ones. He got to eat good every day, except on the road trips like the upcoming one to the Twin Cities.

The arriving players were cordial and thanked Ginny for being so gracious. "Oh, it's nothing. We do this all the time," she said humbly. She used the word "We" but she meant "He!"

They got down to the business of eating almost immediately after everyone arrived. Plates loaded with spaghetti and a few pieces of bread, they headed downstairs to the carpeted TV room, complete with cozy fireplace.

They were talking about the upcoming road games and began eating heartily then the room suddenly became quiet. Worps was in rare form and everyone except the guys who knew Worps from last year was staring at him in amazement.

Reegs looked up from his plate and tapped Tony Denman on the leg "Watch this!" he whispered and motioned towards Worps. Tony's chin dropped in awe as he witnessed the first Worps eating show in Dubuque.

Worps had his hat turned backwards and was shoveling food into his mouth when he noticed the room was quiet and all eyes were glued on him. He looked up making sure not to move his head too far away from his plate. "Whaaa?" Worps said with his mouth fully loaded as he lifted his fork hand up in a puzzled motion. His forked hand was farther away from the plate than he was comfortable with. After a momentary pause he shook his head and continued eating. He knew why they were staring at him; but frankly, he didn't care because he thought it was normal. It was normal...for Worps.

The Worps eating style was legendary. Tod Worpell (Worps) was 5' 10" tall and about 170 pounds, but he eats like a 300 pounder. Worps has the physique of an NFL cornerback, trim and lean, with broad shoulders, a thin waistline and a six-pack abdomen; but he eats like an offensive lineman.

There are only two times when Worps wears his hat backwards. One is when he wants to brag about himself, which is only done in a sarcastic manner. The other time is when he is eating, which happens at least three times a day. If he doesn't turn the hat around while eating, it might get in the way.

Watching Worps eating is quite a thing to witness. The first thing he does after turning his hat around is to gently arrange the plate in close proximity to his head. If the plate is on a table the head will be leaned down close to the plate to provide the shortest possible distance to the mouth. If he is holding the plate in his hand, which was the case in this instance, the same rule applies but his hand brings the plate closer to the head. He holds the fork in the right hand similar to holding a hammer. His eyes are always concentrated straight down at the plate and there will be no time for conversation. Then, once the shoveling hand is furiously set in motion it does not stop until plate is empty. Only then will he lift his head from the plate to pay attention to anything that might be happening around him. He had paused his eating procedure momentarily on this occasion, which was very rare.

"Oh my, I don't think Jim got enough," Ginny thought to herself as she watched Worps shovel more spaghetti into his mouth.

"There's plenty more, Worps," Jim said with a sly grin after Worps completed his first round. He would have a second...and a third, all without interruption. The other guys quickly went back upstairs for seconds as well.

For the last three weeks, the players have been living in the dreary Bluff Street house or the West 11th Street apartments with crappy food. It was nice to partake in a family home with a hearty meal and carpeting. They didn't have carpet at the Bluff Street house. After a plate or two of spaghetti, Gibby and a few others took a nap on the carpeted floor in front of the warm fire. Worps had to kick them awake when it came time to leave.

Later the Denman family and Fallon surveyed the disaster that was the kitchen. All the spaghetti and bread had been eaten. "You were right. I can't believe it...they ate all of it," Ginny was still in awe of whole event.

Jim had a smile on his face as he helped wash the dishes. "This idea was one of my good ones," he thought to himself, and it appeared that he was out of the doghouse.

During the rest of the season, this type of eating event happened regularly. Other families would invite the players over before a weekend series of games for a meal. Sometimes only a few of the guys were invited because some families couldn't handle the whole crew. For some strange reason Worps was always invited. Reegs concluded that the Denman's told everyone they knew about the Worps eating show, and it intrigued so many that they had to see it for themselves.

The legend of Worps was born in Dubuque that night in October of 1980, a day before the season had even started.

Worps was the most unique individual Jack had seen in his long hockey career, and he had seen a large number of young men with some serious issues. In Waterloo, a player short on funds asked Jack for $30 to buy groceries. After Jack gave him the money he bought muskrat traps instead of groceries, thinking he could make enough money on muskrat pelts to survive the season. He didn't survive the week.

Most people in Dubuque thought Worps was a quiet, respectable young man with good manners...except of course when he was eating. That's the way he was when he was out in public or when he was around people he didn't know well. But in the locker room, on the bus and in the house, he was loud and insulting. He was the Saints real life Eddie Haskel.

(Author's note: You young folks may need to Google Eddie Haskel on your smart phones. Go ahead, we'll wait for you.)

Although Worps insulted his teammates at every opportunity, he rarely offended them. It was just a gift he had, similar to Bulldogs scoring skills. It is difficult to explain with words, you needed to experience it in real time. He was never obnoxious or rude, except to Mel on occasion. The players somehow trusted Worps with just about anything. He was a young man with strong ethics, and he would give his right arm for any teammate. Of course, he would only do it after sarcastically telling you what a jerk you are for making him lose his right arm. "Worps is piece of work," Jack would say on multiple occasions.

There was also a third version of Worps...on the ice. When the puck was dropped he was all business. He was not a super skilled player or a great skater but he was one of toughest, hardest working players on the team and was never afraid to "muck it up" along the boards or in the corners where the hard work is usually done. On the ice, he talked loudly only by scoring insane goals and delivering solid body checks.

Jack had selected Mel and Reegs as the Saints official captains, but Worps was the unofficial leader of the team. On the ice he led with his actions. Off the ice he led with sarcasm. The guys needed his weird sense of sarcastic humor to get them through a number of tense situations.

In practices Worps would roll his eyes whenever Jack was talking too much about situations or strategies. On the ice, he had no time for conversation or strategies...it was time to play.

Worps father was a World War II veteran in Europe and met his future wife in France after hostilities ended. They married and moved to Las Vegas where he worked as a child psychologist. The only thing that makes any sense is that Worps was a psychology experiment that went tragically wrong. Worps mother learned English but still had a heavy French accent. Worps would make fun of his mother's accent on a regular basis.

Worps played his youth hockey in Las Vegas, but after his junior year in high school they turned the only hockey arena into a roller-skating rink, essentially ending hockey in Las Vegas. A friend of his had changed his residency to Minnesota to be eligible to play high school hockey several years prior and urged Worps to do the same. Worps moved to Rosemount, Minnesota in 1978. He lived with a friend and his friend's mother in order play high school hockey. Strangely enough Worps friend was one of the guys that did not survive the Cut Locker Room in Dubuque.

October 10th and 11th, 1980:

Saints 6, St Paul 5 (away)

Saints 4, Bloomington 3 (away)

"Nordmark finds a home with Saints" -The Gleaner, Wahlert High School

"Lord, keep my teammates safe tonight. Protect us from physical harm. I ask not for my benefit but for your will. I put my trust in you, oh Lord, I shall not be afraid, for what can mere man do unto me." Jon Nordmark was afraid. Before every game he said a similar prayer to overcome his fear. It was one of the reasons he came back to the team when all the advice he was getting told him otherwise.

Jon Nordmark (Nordsy) was a 17-year-old high school senior from Westminster Colorado. Jon was 5' 9" tall, 170 pounds and had curly blond hair. In Colorado Nordsy was one of the best players in the state at his age. He was named MVP four times in his four years of advanced youth hockey. Bob Johnson, the coach for the University of Wisconsin Badgers, saw Nordsy play in Colorado and convinced him to tryout for the Dubuque Fighting Saints.

Nordmark was one of the few Saints players that had never been cut, but when he saw the talent level during tryouts he thought this would probably be his first. "I thought I would be lucky to make this team," recalled Nordmark. After the tryout sessions Nordmark was still on the team. Then came the Elmhurst preseason games. Nordsy's parents flew in to Dubuque to witness both preseason games against the Huskies. They were not impressed, to say the least. During the home game Jon received a butt-end that bruised his face and his eyelids were almost swollen shut. Nordsy made the team after that game, his record of never being cut was still intact, but his parents wanted to take him home immediately, and they did. They told their son that he needed to attend his high school homecoming activities back in Colorado, and then they would talk him out of returning to Dubuque. They also enlisted the help of Jon's Colorado friends, hoping they would convince him to stay home.

Back in Colorado, Nordsy was conflicted, "How can I leave this team with so much talent?" he asked himself. Then he answered, "I can't. It's that simple, I just can't." For the first time in his life he wouldn't be the best player on the team. In fact, he would probably be on the third line. One of the other things that compelled him to go back was the fear; he had to conquer that fear. Something inside told him that he could not run away from it. He told his parents, "This is a personal challenge...I have to go back."

At the airport, he told his mother, "Mom, you have to understand, this is something I have to do. I'll be fine Mom. I like these guys. They will take care of me." The last part did not install any confidence in his mother. She cried openly as he walked toward the gate. He boarded a flight to St. Paul to catch up with the team for the first game of the season.

Nordsy fought back the fear in St. Paul and in Bloomington with the help of prayer. When the puck dropped the fear was gone. Nordsy played his own style of hockey. He went full speed ahead with reckless abandon until the whistle blew or the puck went in the opposing net. It was this style of play and his skating ability that impressed Bob Johnson. Nordsy would play that way all season long.

Towards the end of the Bloomington game, Nordsy was back-checking an opposing player into the defending zone. He let the guy get a step on him from a momentary lapse of judgment. The guy got into the open, took a pass and scored a goal that brought the Bloomington Junior Stars to within one goal of tying the game.

Nordmark came back to bench dejected. He braced himself for the criticism he had just earned, but Barzee said nothing. Jack knew that Nordsy would be hard on himself and anything he could say would only make it worse. As Coach Jack knew that at times like this his silence was the best motivational tool he could use.

"Next time you'll get him, that is your only option," said Worps.

"Don't worry about it, we'll pop a few more in," said Collins.

It was then that Nordsy knew he had made the right decision to come back. "These guys were propping me up when I deserved to be cut down," he thought to himself. "These are the most amazing bunch of guys I will ever play the game with! I hope I can live up to their standards."

October 16ᵗʰ, 1980:

Saints 9, Des Moines 4 (home)

"Three goals in 45 seconds spark Fighting Saints" -Telegraph Herald

When the players moved into the house on Bluff Street, it was mostly unfurnished. Almost all the rooms had mattresses but no bed frames, so the mattresses sat on the floor. If you were one of the lucky ones, you had a mattress on a box spring on a floor.

The furnishings consisted of a stove and a refrigerator in the kitchen, but there was little else to speak of. Gibby kept his beer tapper fridge in the room he shared with Worps. The beer tapper was rarely used. Mostly, it was filled with milk and food. As veterans of life in the USHL, Gibby and Worps kept their milk in their own fridge. They never seemed to have milk when they needed it. Each person would have his own area in the fridge, but somehow Gibby's milk would always magically dwindle down to nothing. When you live in a house with eight other guys that tends to happen. At some point Gibby had enough of the milk thievery. He came up with a tracking method of squeezing some shampoo into his milk container in the main refrigerator.

That night, as normal, they all made separate meals. The word "meals" might be misleading as they only consisted of Stovetop stuffing, Ramen noodles, or macaroni & cheese. One of the guys said he could not finish his Mac & Cheese and handed the remnants to Worps. Worps was about to dig in when he noticed a distinct soapy smell. "How could you eat this?" he said. Gibby's milk tracking method worked and the thief was caught.

One of the amenities they enjoyed was a large screen TV, 32 inches. That was a large screen in 1980. It was a big "tube" model with a wooden case and four 12-inch legs, which provided the perfect viewing height. Just like Worps, this TV had problems. The picture began to slant. The whole picture tilted inside the tube. Each day the slant would grow worse. It's like hitting the rotate button for rotating a picture on a modern computer. It started out at about 10 degrees angle and by the end of the month it was at 40 degrees. This cut off the corners of the picture. Undeterred, the guys continued to watch the TV with their heads tilted. Finally, with a sore neck, Badger couldn't take it anymore. Once again he solved a complex problem with a common sense solution. He cleared the junk off the top of the TV and removed the two legs on one side. The picture was now level even if the actual TV was slanted. It looked awkward and if you set anything on the TV it would immediately slide off, but the problem was solved, at least for the time being.

They continued to watch a lot on that TV. They watched sitcoms, they watched football games, and they even watched President Reagan get shot on that tilted TV. But mostly they watched Soap Operas. Ryan's Hope, All My Children and General Hospital were the favorites. The TV kept getting worse and the situation became dire for Worps. Worps was one of the guys that had a night job during the week. He was a gym supervisor at recreation basketball games. He got the courts ready and was supposed to make sure things never got out of hand. During the day he watched soap operas, and now he was beside himself.

Three working girls in their early twenties lived next door, and they had a nice TV. Their names were Laurie, Shelly, and Julie. Worps didn't know how to ask them to leave their door unlocked so he could watch Soap Operas during the day. Once again it was Badger to the rescue. Why these young ladies would let strange men roam freely in their home while they were at work is beyond comprehension, but somehow Badger convinced them it would be ok. Each day Worps would ask Badger to ask the ladies for permission. Eventually Badger refused, so Worps summoned the courage to ask each day until the ladies got tired of the begging and left the door open. The ladies were not big hockey fans, but somehow the guys earned their trust. The ladies started going to the games more regularly and they soon became hockey fans and good friends with the guys on Bluff Street.

October 19th, 1980:

Saints 11, Black Hawks 4 (home)

"Motzko's four goals lead Saints to fourth straight victory" -*Telegraph Herald*

It was the typical busy day for Badger and Gibby. After the morning practice they got home by eleven, just in time to catch a half hour of Ryan's Hope while they ate breakfast. By noon they were at work at Frommelt Industries and worked until the end of the shift at 5p.m.

"You going to the Walnut tonight?" Badger said on the way home. Some of the Bluff Street guys were planning on going to the Walnut Tap to shoot pool with Deano and Collins.

"Nope, frikking Jack volunteered me for public skating again," Gibby said. The players regularly "volunteered" to help out with the nightly public skating sessions at the Five Flags. Most of them liked the opportunity to meet and mingle with the people of Dubuque. The young kids also liked having the chance to skate with the players.

Dubuque was now Jack Barzee's home, so he had a vested interest in the development of the community and its youth, but it was also an opportunity to sell seats by presenting a good public image and community interaction. At the time, Gibby just thought Jack was trying to keep him out of the bars.

"I gotta sharpen some skates so maybe I'll see ya at the rink," Badger said as they got home.

After a quick meal of Mac and Cheese, Gibby put on his Hartford Whalers hat and took the block and half walk to the Five Flags. Inside the locker room he tied his skates loosely to keep them comfortable for the slow monotonous skating. He almost never tied his skates comfortably, but this was different. Public skating sessions are notoriously boring affairs of skating in circles. Those in charge never let anyone skate too fast as it would endanger the slower skaters. They had safety rules that needed to be enforced. The players liked it when they had to chase down a delinquent kid that was skating too fast, because it also allowed them to skate fast. They figured some of these kids did it on purpose to see how long they could evade a "Saint" before being captured and sent off the ice. It was all in good fun. Thankfully, the rules were less stringent at the Five Flags than they were at places back in Minnesota.

"Your skates are too loose," Gibby said to an 8-year-old when he caught him in their game of cat and mouse.

"My mom dropped me off and I tied them myself," said the youngster struggling to break free as Gibby dragged him off the ice.

Gibby sat him down in one of the chairs lined up along the boards just off the ice. "You need to have these as tight as you can if you are going to be fast out there," he said as he proceeded to re-tighten the boy's skates.

Most hockey players want their skates as tight as possible. For many this caused an injury called "Lace Bite" where the pressure of the laces combined with the weight and push of a skating stride would make the laces damage the tendons just above the ankle. Lace Bite caused great pain and sometimes made players have to sit out days or weeks to allow the healing process to complete. Some never healed and they played through constant pain.

Gibby had skates that were two sizes too small. He wanted the smallest skates possible for maneuverability and quickness, and they had to be tight to act as an extension of the leg. For him the act of tying his skates was a workout by itself. He would pull and tug and hold one lace while he tugged on the other. He would be winded by the time he was finished. For some unknown reason, he rarely got Lace Bite.

Badger came out of the locker room after sharpening skates. "I see you are finally doing something you're good at," he said ribbing Gibby about tying the young boys skates.

Gibby acknowledged Badger. "Hey Badge, can you watch the rink for a minute while I tie these? And make sure no one exceeds the speed limit." Gibby added the last part sarcastically.

That is when it happened. Badger watched as a 12-year-old girl was trying to do a figure skating spin maneuver. She wiped-out. A fall on the ice in itself is not a big deal as they happened all the time at public skating sessions. Most kids get right back up and keep skating or come back to the door crying with their ego hurting worse than any body parts.

This was different. This girl was not getting up, and she was clutching her leg. Badger walked out onto the ice in his shoes to assess the situation. The girl was frantically crying but was able to tell Badger that her left leg was hurt badly.

Badger calmed her down then picked her up and carried her to the chairs and set her down gently near Gibby and the 8-year-old boy. Badger looked her leg over and saw that she had a cut in her skating tights a couple inches above the knee with a little bit of blood dripping out.

"Does it still hurt or just when you move it?" Badger asked the sniffling young girl.

"I think it's better now," she paused and then bent her leg to about 90 degrees at the knee. As she did this a geyser of blood spewed out of the wound above her knee, gushing up like a crimson drinking fountain, at least 6 inches high.

The quick-thinking Badger reached up to the girls face and aggressively turned her head away. He also quickly straightened out her leg.

It was a nasty site to see. Blood was everywhere on Badgers hands and dripping on the floor. Gibby had seen a lot of blood playing hockey but never a fountain of blood like that. He started to feel nauseous.

Thankfully Badger took charge. "Hey," he said to an older boy drawn in by the commotion. "Go out front and get someone to call an ambulance." Gibby had his skates on so he was of no use, not to mention his face was turning an odd shade of green.

"You look like a good skater. Do you skate here a lot?" Badger was diverting the young girl's mind away from the injury to keep her calm. It worked on Gibby as well.

"Are your parents around?" Badger asked the girl.

"They're at home. I think one of my friends went to call them," she answered.

Badger contemplated driving her to the hospital himself, but the "Boat" was a block and a half away. Eventually the older boy returned with the girl's parents and the paramedics arrived to take control of the situation.

During the fall the girl stabbed the heel of her figure skate blade into her lower thigh. Apparently, the cut was deep enough to sever a main artery in her leg. The wound required surgery at the hospital, but the girl remained amazingly calm throughout the ordeal.

When they got back to the house Gibby asked, "Why did you turn her head like that?"

"I didn't want her to panic...like you did," said Badger. He was obviously well trained in first aid and it paid off.

Gibby was reliving the incident in his mind. "Oh yah, I forgot about the boy's skates I was tying...I hope he didn't see that blood gusher. I'm gonna have nightmares for weeks!"

October 25th and 26th, 1980:

Saints 6, Austin 4 (home)

Saints 2, Austin 1 (away)

"Four goals in first period spark Saints to fifth straight win" -*Telegraph Herald*

After the departure of Cookie, Lex, Fielding and Glickman, the team was short 4 players on the normal 20-man roster. Jack was not a big fan of having extra players on the roster that would not see much ice time. This was a developmental league. If a player is not getting regular ice time, it is best to let them find another place to develop their skills.

Even though John Lex left the team, Jack still owned his rights to play in the league. Looking for another goalie, Jack shopped the talented John Lex rights to Bloomington for Brian Granger.

Brian Granger stood 5 feet 11 inches tall, 175 pounds and took up a lot of the net. He was a stand-up goalie. Goalies today tend to drop to their knees on every shot. Granger held his ground and rarely gave up the top corners of the net. Granger graduated from Bloomington Jefferson High School in Minnesota the year before, tried out for the Bloomington Junior Stars and made the team before being traded to Dubuque. Granger moved in with Walshy in one of the 11th Street apartments.

Jack brought Granger in and put him into the games right away, helping to relieve some of the pressure on Jask. Granger and Jask would share Saints goaltending duties for the rest of the season.

Glenn Scanlan (Scanny) came over from Waterloo in late October. The Black Hawks released him outright and the Saints needed another forward. Scanny could play forward or defense and was willing to do anything to make the team. The 6 foot 180 pound sandy haired blonde went to Waterloo from Lawrence, New Jersey looking for a place to play competitive hockey.

Scanny worked hard in practice and games, but he was not one of the more talented players. He saw limited playing time, with Jack spotting him in at forward and defense through the first half of the season. Jack's plan was to keep Scanny as the player that would step in when the inevitable season ending injury happened. Unfortunately for Scanny, that type of injury never happened during the Saints season. However, there were plenty of day-to-day injuries and game ejections where Scanny was able to effectively fill in at any position, except goalie.

Scanny was liked by all his teammates and rarely complained about his role as a fill-in player. When he did make light of it he would do it in a humorous way, keeping it light hearted. Scanny had a special humor that complimented Worps' sarcastic insults in the locker room and on the bus rides.

Later in the season, Scanny's parents made the trip to Dubuque to check up on their son. He wrote home earlier saying everything was fine, but they didn't believe him. After arriving and seeing that he was, in fact, just fine as his letters stated, the Scanlan parents tried to find adventures in Dubuque. One thing they had never done was to walk across the Mississippi River. Not across the bridge, mind you, but across the floating ice.

The Mississippi River does not always freeze solid in the winter in Dubuque. Trying to walk across the river is a bad idea. Most people said it was suicidal.

"Do you have your life insurance current?" Scanny asked of his parents before they set out on their journey. Scanny did not accompany them to their departure point. In fact, no one was there to rescue them if they got stranded...or worse. The first fifty yards or so was solid, but then they had to hold hands and jump across openings from floating ice chunk to the next. When they got to solid ice on the other side, they gave each other a long hug and then continued up the embankment to the road. They played it safe by walking back to Dubuque over the bridge. This incident possibly explains some of Scanny's personality issues: they say the apple does not fall far from the tree.

Scanny was one of the friendliest guys on the team. Good natured and slow to anger, he fit in good with Deano and Collins. Scanny asked them if they had room in the 11th Street apartment for a "3rd wheel." "Sure, why not," Deano said. Deano, Collins and Scanny made a great trio in Dubuque, but it wouldn't last. Scanny always felt that his time in Dubuque would be limited.

November 1st and 2nd, 1980:

Saints 9, Des Moines 6 (away)

Green Bay 9, Saints 8 (home)

"Green Bay's overtime efforts ends Saints winning streak" - Telegraph Herald

Racing after the puck the linesman blew his whistle to complete an icing call. George Beavs, Jr. picked up the puck and raced back to hand it to the other linesman waiting at the end of the rink. He didn't have to go fast because the play was blown dead by the whistle, but he liked skating fast. It was one of the reasons these local Dubuque guys became linesmen in the first place; they loved to skate. Now, they actually get paid to skate.

Al Stoltz (Stoltzy) didn't have to wait long for his partner to bring him the puck. Beavs was coming in fast, too fast. Beavs tried to stop but caught an edge and fell to the ice just as he arrived. His momentum took out Stoltzy's legs and sent him flying into the air, landing with a thud right on the faceoff dot as players scurried for cover. Beavs ended up in the corner still holding the puck as eighteen hundred fans were cheering and laughing. From the bench TD Feldman laughed loudly, as he joined the crowd and the players in clapping. Beavs picked himself up, shook off the snow, handed the puck to the now upright Stoltzy and took his place outside the faceoff zone with his pride still intact.

Earlier in the fall, four local Dubuque young men made the trip to Madison to become AHAUS certified to officiate youth hockey games. In Madison, they went over the duties of the linesman: offside, icing, hand passes, playing the puck with a high stick, ensuring the proper number of on-ice players, proper positioning, and conducting face-offs. At the time, this was all that was required to be a linesman in the USHL. There were a few other duties they did not cover such as equipment violations, reporting major penalties and breaking up fights. The last one they had to learn through experience.

Stoltzy, Mike Waddick (Waddy), George Beavs, Jr. and Jay Imhofe would share the linesman assignments. Stoltzy and Waddy had already gotten through several rough games where they had to break up fights, including the preseason Elmhurst Huskie fiasco. They officiated that game for free to get some experience. Barzee felt guilty about all the fights they had to break up so he gave them both a used pair of hockey gloves as a bonus.

Waddy was 24 at the time and recently returned from a three-year enlistment in the Army. He was still a little rough around the edges and sported a scruffy beard. He played hockey outdoors at Flora Park whenever he could. He soon found himself organizing the adult hockey league, which by 1980 had six teams and a full schedule of indoor games at the Five Flags Center.

Stoltzy was a clean-cut innocent boy reminiscent of Richie Cunningham from Happy Days except Stoltzy was six foot two with dark hair. (Author's Note: Ok kids, go ahead and Google Happy Days on your smart phone, or better yet, give this book to your mother. You probably shouldn't be reading it anyway.)

Waddy and Stoltzy invited a few of the players to go pheasant hunting in the fall. Bulldog, Grillo and Badger took them up on the offer.

"Badger was probably the worst pheasant hunter ever. He 'hip' shot his first bird from about 15 feet and blew it to pieces!" said Stoltzy.

"That's a pretty good shot if you ask me," said Grillo in Badger's defense. They shot several birds without shooting each other, so the hunt was considered a success.

Sometime later Scanny was invited on one of these bird hunts. Scanny had no experience with bird hunting and very little experience with guns. Collins gave Scanny his spare shotgun then they packed into Deano's truck and wandered aimlessly in search of pheasants. They stopped along the road and wandered into a farmer's field without asking permission. Collins gave Scanny one shell and showed him how to load and unload the gun. "You only need one shell. Anymore and you'll be a danger to everyone else," said Collins seriously. They saw a few pheasants but Scanny never got a chance to pull the trigger. He saw a rabbit but they were not hunting rabbits. After more walking Scanny put his shotgun shell in his pocket. It felt safer that way. He was pretty sure he wouldn't be able to hit anything anyway.

As they were walking back to the truck, Scanny noticed the rabbit again but this time it was closer. "Can I shoot a rabbit?" Scanny asked.

"You can shoot anything you are going to eat," Collins replied.

Like Barney Fife in the Andy Griffith show, Scanny reached into his pocket, pulled out his lone shotgun shell, loaded it into the gun, chambered the round and looked up to see that the rabbit was holding still. Ka-boom! After Scanny opened his eyes he saw the rabbit was not dead. It was in the field flailing, and then it let out a loud screech. Mortified, Scanny walked up to it, but he had no more ammunition. He had to dispatch the rabbit with the butt of his shotgun.

Already feeling extremely depressed, Scanny had to carry the rabbit in the front pocket of his sweatshirt, the blood soaking through as Deano and Collins continued hunting. They stopped the truck in another field after spotting a rooster. Deano hopped out of the truck, loaded his gun and ran after the pheasant. He shot it as it got up to fly away. On his way back a farmer chased Deano out of the field while screaming at him. Deano came running back to the truck at full speed, threw the dead pheasant in the back, hopped in and peeled out before the farmer could catch up to them.

Back at the 11th Street apartment, Deano and Collins made Scanny go outside to clean his kill. Scanny discovered that rabbits were mostly made of fur and smelled like the inside of a skunk. He put the skinny little carcass in a brown paper bag and put it in the freezer. He wanted to fulfill his obligation to eat what he shot, but he couldn't do it. Scanny was mentally scarred from killing the poor animal; he was not going to add emotional and possible physical damage by eating it. Scanny left it in the freezer when they vacated the apartment at the end of the season. "Maybe someone who moves in next will eat it," he hoped.

November 8ᵗʰ and 12ᵗʰ, 1980:

Saints 10, Bloomington 2 (home)

Saints 5, Bloomington 4 (away)

"Saints rout Bloomington in penalty-filled contest" -*Telegraph Herald*

Fighting was regular entertainment for Saints fans. It wasn't entertainment for Stoltzy and Waddy; they took it seriously. Despite having no training or process to break up fights, they approached the job aggressively. Well, at least Waddy did. Early in the season he got a little too physical with a Waterloo player while breaking up a fight. He pulled the player down with too much force and landed on top of him, separating the player's shoulder. That player was out of action for six weeks.

"I'll be waiting for you outside!" Mark Lescarbeau, the Waterloo captain, threatened Waddy after the game ended. The Black Hawk captain rightfully blamed Waddy for the injury and wanted revenge. Waddy took his time in the shower, folded his sweaty clothes then waited some extra time before making his way out into the lobby. When he walked out to his car the vengeful Black Hawk captain had left with the bus, just as Waddy planned.

Throughout the year breaking up a fight was as physically exhausting as it was dangerous for the linesmen. A missed punch could hit a linesman at any time so they had to wait for the players to stop swinging or go to the ice before jumping in to break it up. They didn't know it at the time, but linesmen are supposed to grab opposing players at the same time to prevent one from getting a "free shot" at a defenseless player. This happened on occasion.

Back in 1980 the officials did not wear helmets, so there was not only danger from fists and pucks but also the possibility of hitting your head on the ice. In Waddy's officiating career he needed 21 stitches to repair damage to his head, face and hands. Compare that to Gibby who was a player for two and half years in the USHL, got in more than 15 fights, blocked countless shots but never required a stitch.

As local officials, Stoltzy and Waddy were not celebrities. In fact, they were regularly heckled and frowned upon. A majority, if not all hockey officials are impartial by instinct. They would never screw up a call on purpose. Oh yes, they would regularly screw up calls, just not intentionally. The game is fast and they are human, so they are bound to make mistakes. Sometimes the fans can get a little too emotional about a call, especially the home crowd, on a hometown official.

A fan was continually screaming at Waddy during the game against Bloomington, even though the Saints continually dominated. It was clear the guy had too much to drink. The fan continued to scream at Waddy as he came off the ice at the end of the game. Once again Waddy took his time in the shower to give the drunken fan time to leave before he went through the lobby. This time, however, the fan was still there, and he appeared to be waiting for Waddy.

Waddy knew he would be kicked out of the league if he fought with a fan inside the arena, so he put his head down and quickly walked by the unruly fan. Unfortunately, the fan followed him out of the arena.

As Waddy got to his car, he figured he was far enough away from the arena to absolve him of any responsibility. He threw his bag into the back seat and took a quick step towards the drunken fan, hoping to catch him off guard.

"Alright you son of a bitch, I'm gonna beat the shit out of you! Let's get it done with right now!"

The guy stepped back a few steps and put his hands up, "Hold on a second man. I'm really drunk and shouldn't have said those things. I just wanted to apologize."

November 14th and 15th, 1980:

Saints 3, St. Paul 2 (away)
Sioux City 6, Saints 5 (away)

"Saints lose at Sioux City after 3-2 win over Vulcans" -Telegraph Herald

"Can someone tell me again why we are leaving tonight?" said Worps. The guys were in the locker room after practice talking about the upcoming St. Paul-Sioux City road trip. Jack scheduled the bus to leave at 10 p.m. the night before the first game to avoid bus-legs when they played St. Paul the following day. Jack wanted the team to stay in a hotel room near the arena so they would be rested for the game the next day. There was a flaw in Jack's plan. To be rested the next day you generally don't want to arrive at your destination at two in the morning.

The guys left the locker room and went about their normal daily routines. When Gibby and Badger got home from work, Worps told them he was heading to the Walnut for a little "pre-trip" activity.

"What the heck, it can't hurt anything. We aren't playing until tomorrow," Worps rationalized. He advised the guys to pack their bags before they went to the Walnut. Worps, Gibby and Grillo arrived at the Walnut at 7 p.m. The bus wasn't leaving for another three hours, plenty of time to have a few beers and catch the bus on time.

A lot of the guys from the 11th Street apartments were at the Walnut before the Bluff Street guys arrived. They shot pool and drank some beer. Then some fans showed up and started buying pitchers of beer. As time to leave drew near a few of the guys left to pack their bags and get ready for the trip. "We should probably get going," said Grillo. At that point Collins went behind the bar and made a phone call to the rink. He arranged for TD and Badger to load their bags onto the bus and Clarence, the "good-guy" bus driver, would stop the bus in front of the Walnut to pick them up.

Clarence was nicknamed the "good-guy" bus driver by the players. He allowed the team to bend the rules and have a little fun on the bus. He was also a friendly guy in his late forties that joked and laughed with the players. Clarence was a good guy.

The "bad-guy" bus driver was always crabby and rarely talked with the players. The only time he spoke to the players was to yell at them for breaking some rule. He was a curmudgeon. It seemed like the bus company had only two bus drivers...the good guy and the bad guy. One or the other drove the bus on all the road trips.

"Three cheers for Collins!" Grillo blurted out and raised his glass.

"Three cheers for Clarence!" Collins yelled back.

The bus pulled up in front of the Walnut and the guys piled on. Trying not to draw attention, Worps kept quiet, which was a monumental feat for him. By the time they arrived in St. Paul, they were hung over and thirsty. They got to their rooms, drank pitchers of water and then went to bed.

They beat St. Paul 3-2 and stayed in the same hotel before heading to Sioux City in the morning. Sioux City was always a terrible place to play. The rink was an ancient theater that was turned into a hockey arena. There was not enough room for a hockey arena, so they cut corners. The visiting locker room was up a flight of metal stairs; the players benches went perpendicular to the rink through one of the bleacher exits. Only the two players on the end of the bench could see the ice and watch the game. The ice surface was only 165 feet long, 20 feet shorter than most rinks and 35 feet shorter than others. When you carried the puck over the center red line, you could take a shot with a reasonable expectation that you could score.

In between periods the guys did not want to walk up the metal stairs so they had chairs set up on the stage behind the curtain. Scanny would regularly entertain the team by playing the Peanuts theme and other songs on the piano. Scanny was an accomplished piano player. The guys were impressed that he could run the leg apparatus with his skates on.

Back on the bench during the game, the guys sat there not knowing what was going on in the game and occasionally getting beers poured on them from the fans. There was chicken wire above the bench to prevent fans from throwing harmful items at the players but that did not stop beer, the regular verbal assaults, or the "finger" from Musketeer fans. Worps suggested that they did nuclear experiments around Sioux City, then sent the people who were affected the worst by radiation to the games, and gave them beer.

The Saints got beat by Sioux City 6-5. After the game most of the guys quietly took their skates off on the stage carrying them up to the locker room. Worps and a few others walked up the metal steps making a loud clanking noise not caring if it ruined their blades.

The showers were the worst experience of the trip. The Sioux City locker room had 4 showers, but only one worked and it shot a laser beam of water that would burn into your skin. The guys would lather up and then designate one person to deflect the water laser beam. The "deflector" held a piece of cardboard over the laser beam, slowing the water down and dispersing the water so they could rinse off.

This was the first time most of the guys played on the short ice surface. It was clear they would have to make adjustments in future games. This is one game the Saints should have easily won, but they let it slip away.

The Bulldog line: Bulldog (right), Collins (middle), Deano (Left)

November 19th, 1980:

Saints 11, Waterloo 7 (home)

"Thomas, Collins lead Saints to 11-7 victory" -*Telegraph Herald*

Skating hard for the puck, Deano fell and slid into boards. He was going full speed when he hit the bottom of the boards, the least forgiving part. He skated back to the bench slowly with a puzzled look on his face, holding his right hand.

TD immediately knew something was wrong and met him as he came off the ice. There was no sign of pain on Deano's face as he slid his glove off slowly. "Does it hurt?" TD asked.

"Not really, but I don't think it's supposed to bend like that," Deano calmly replied. Deano's thumb was pointing the wrong direction.

TD laughed at Deano's comment as he felt the bone structure around his thumb. "Does it hurt right here?" he asked again and pressed lightly on the main joint connecting the thumb.

"A little," Deano said.

"Hold your arm still," TD ordered. Then he slammed Deano's thumb back into its socket.

"OWWW! Son of a bitch! ...It hurts now!" Deano screamed.

"It was dislocated," TD correctly diagnosed. "I'll tape it up so you can finish the game, but you're going to have to go see Doc Field tomorrow and get it X-rayed."

The next day Deano came to the rink with a cast on his right hand. Jack was worried that he may have lost one of his top scorers for weeks or months, but Deano assured him that he could play with the cast on. Doc Field said it was not broken, just badly dislocated; he wanted to have the cast on for 3-4 weeks.

Later in the week two young ladies walked into the Avenue Tap bar on University Avenue looking to unwind after a long day of work at the Mercy Hospital. "Isn't that one of those hockey players you were talking about?" Christy said to Donna.

Christy was an unattached petite 22-year-old blonde with a friendly smile. She worked as a Respiratory Therapist. Donna was a 23-year-old with long brown hair. She worked as a nurse in Doc Fields office.

"Yes, that's Brian Collins," Donna replied. Early in the season Doc Field asked some of the nurses to take the players out and show them the town. He said the guys don't know anyone in town, and they need some local friends to hang out with.

The ladies wandered over to Brian Collins and introduced themselves. They got straight to the point. "There's a party on Friday if you and some of the hockey players want go with us?"

After a while the ladies came to the realization that giving Collins the address would be useless because these guys had no way of knowing how to get around the maze of twisting Dubuque streets. The ladies agreed to pick up the guys and bring them to the party. (Author's note: Remember kids, if you're still reading this, they didn't have GPS phones back then).

On Friday they stopped at the 11th Street apartments and picked up Collins. Deano, Bucky and Scanny would follow in Deano's truck. "Four guys will be manageable," thought Christy.

"We need to run by the Bluff Street house to get some of those guys," said Collins.

When they stopped on Bluff Street, eight players came out of the house and walked up to the car.

"Umm...all of them?" Christy was uneasy with that many people, but she and Donna never set a limit on the number of guys they were inviting to the party.

"Not a problem," said Collins. "Gibby's got a big car. He can follow in the Boat." The three-car caravan slowly made its way to the party with a total of twelve teammates.

There were a lot of people at the party. Most of the ladies were happy to see the hockey players, but most of the local guys were not too keen about it, for obvious reasons.

Christy was keeping a close eye on Deano. She saw him walk into the kitchen area and start digging through the drawers. When Christy walked into the kitchen the two were alone. Deano found a sharp pair of scissors and was struggling to cut the cast off his hand. He asked Christy for some help. Being a health care professional Christy strongly advised against it, but Deano's hand was itching so bad it was driving him crazy. Together they strategically cut the cast in half so it could be put back on when needed. "Don't tell anyone I helped you do this," she told Deano.

As the night got late, Donna wanted to go home. "Here, just take the car, I'll find a ride," Christy told her friend and handed her the keys. She made her way over to Deano and told him that she needed a ride home because Donna took her car. It was a sly move, but it worked. Deano gave Christy a ride home in his truck and the rest of the guys piled into Gibby's big red boat.

Later, Christy started going to the Saints games and learned a little more about hockey from Deano. They eventually went on real dates and became a couple for the rest of the season. When Donna later asked Christy about her choice of players, she replied, "Dean Thomas is good looking and he's on the first line. I don't want to date a second or third liner."

November 23rd, 1980:

Saints 10, St. Paul 8 (home)

"Five Flags - A place to vent frustrations" -Hal Lagerstrom, Telegraph Herald

On Bluff Street, the guys were relaxing in the living room watching football on the slanted TV. It was a relatively cold Sunday afternoon and none of the guys had to work at their day jobs.

Contrary to popular belief at the time, the players were not paid to play hockey in Dubuque. In fact, most of the players barely made ends meet by working menial jobs supplanted with occasional stipends from parents. Many of the part time jobs were as janitors or laborers. Jask and Collins worked at the power company doing janitorial work. Bucky and Vogy washed trucks at a local trucking company. Deano and Scanny wiped down cars at Miracle Car Wash. Bulldog worked at Montgomery Wards in the automotive department doing tire installs. Chris Guy worked at a gas station. Gibby and Badger worked at Frommelt Industries as laborers.

Bucky was on the job one day in late November when several coworkers ran by heading for the truck scales and yelling for him to grab a pitchfork. Frightened and unsure what to do, Bucky followed, forgetting to arm himself with a pitchfork. The men were lining up between the Mississippi river and the truck scales. Bucky stood behind a line of men with pitchforks when the order came to lift the scales. As soon as the scales lifted, thousands of rats began scurrying for the river. Men were stabbing at the ground as the rats ran by. The men stationed near the scales were the busiest. In horror, Bucky backed away trying to keep the others from stabbing him in the foot.

Some of the guys had more glamorous jobs. Fallon and Reegs worked for Jim Denman at Oak Ridge Sports. Walshy worked at Marting Shoe Store selling shoes. Nordsy was still in high school and he took his education seriously. Unlike Fallon, Nordsy actually studied during his down time from hockey. Granger was supposed to work at the ski hill in town but it was a warm winter and didn't snow very much, so he was not needed there. He saved money by using his bicycle for transportation.

Grillo saved up enough money during the previous summer to avoid work altogether. He slept late and watched soap's with Worps during the day. Worps had the cushiest job of all. He was a Gym Supervisor in the evenings during adult league basketball games. His duties included getting the balls out before the games and putting them back afterwards, in addition to making sure no fans got out of hand.

Worps said, "You guys have to see Larry. He's my idol. Every time he shoots a basket, he looks up into the bleachers to see if people are watching. Larry is awesome!"

Worps convinced several of the guys to go to the gym to watch Larry play basketball. Sure enough, every time he took a shot he looked up into the stands. The guys let him know they were watching by cheering him on. The cheering was the loudest when he was successful and they booed when he missed. Larry did not know the group of six strangers came there just to watch him. Initially, the guys were cheering sarcastically but by the end they were truly rooting for him. Booing is not as much fun as cheering. Larry cemented his place as an idol for the rest of the season, but the guys never went back to watch him. It was more fun to hear Worps tell the stories when he got home from work.

Gibby and Badger got laid off from Frommelt Industries just before Christmas. Gibby became a Gym Supervisor in Sageville and Badger went to work with Mel at the YMCA. Mel worked at the YMCA helping in the weight room and other areas.

Back in the Bluff Street living room, the topic of discussion turned to Mel. "Hey Mel, I heard you're going to enter into the Tough Man Contest?" Worps lied. He was egging Mel on because he heard that people were saying Mel could easily win. The Tough Man Contest was basically the precursor to todays mixed martial arts contests, except that they only allowed amateurs to step into the ring. These events were being held throughout the country. The second annual tri-state Tough Man contest was going to be held at the Five Flags Center in Dubuque on December 12th and 13th. The winner would get $1000, the runner up would get $500 and both moved on to the region match and get a chance at the national title.

It was true that many of the hockey fans were asking for Mel to enter the contest. Mel was considering it, but on the second night of contest the Saints would be in Green Bay which meant that Mel would miss out on the championship, if he made it that far. Barzee might have had something to say about it as well.

Mel grunted and shook his head but said nothing in response. "I'll take that as a No," said Worps. Worps egged him on further but Mel kept quiet. The fact of the matter is that last year's winner was an ex-golden glove boxer who weighed in at 230 pounds and he beat a University of Dubuque offensive lineman and national wrestling champion that weighed over 260 pounds. Mel was extremely tough in a hockey fight, but he might have been over-matched against that type of competition.

November 26th, 1980:

Des Moines 6, Saints 4 (away)

"Fighting Saints fall, 6-4" -*Telegraph Herald*

The day before the away game against the hated Des Moines Buccaneers, they went to Oak Ridge Sports to check out the new supply of sticks Jim Denman had in stock. The Saints organization supplied hockey sticks for the players, but those sticks were always the cheaper ones and Jack put restrictions on how many a player would get. None of them actually had money to buy the sticks, but they could look and dream at the sporting goods store.

They mulled around for an hour before Reegs decided it was time to go. "Let's go guys," Reegs said as he corralled the seven Saints players towards the exit. He didn't want to stay too long since they weren't paying customers.

Seated comfortably in Gibby's big red "Boat" for the trip home was a quarter of the Saints roster. Grillo and Bulldog were seated in the front seat with Gibby driving. Worps, Badger, Guy, and Reegs were in the back.

They were traveling well over the speed limit coming down the hill on Dodge Street towards the busy University Avenue intersection when the light turned red. Gibby applied brake pressure and heard a clunking noise, and then the brake pedal went to the floor.

"We're screwed!" Gibby yelled.

At first they thought it was one of Gibby's bad jokes but seeing the fear on his face told them otherwise. He was pumping furiously on the pedal but they were not slowing down. "We're going in!" Gibby shouted.

Bulldog opened the door and contemplated rolling out. He closed the door after seeing the speed of the pavement rushing underneath. "Better to take your chances inside the Boat," Bulldog quickly concluded.

They went through the red light, merged into oncoming traffic, fitting neatly in between a turning car and a big truck. The truck honked his horn and flipped them off as he sped past them on the uphill side of the intersection.

Gibby continued to pump the brakes and eventually pressure returned. The guys were relieved but still worried about the trip back to Bluff Street. Gibby inched along, making sure he had brakes to stop or a road to the right for a safe exit.

When they made it home safely Bulldog got out and kissed the ground. A collision at that intersection, at the speed they were going with the car full of players, could have ended the season for the Saints.

Gibby never knew what parts fell off the Boat. He topped off the brake fluid and the brakes worked for the rest of the season, but he never trusted them. He started wearing a helmet in addition to his seat belt. He rarely carried that many players in the car again, mainly because the guys found safer means of transportation.

Worps started driving his $25 car more often. Bulldog even used his Dodge Dart. One night after an extended stay at the Walnut Tap, the guys were afraid that Bulldog had drunk too much to drive them home safely.

"It's not safe!" said Worps. "I think it's safer on the outside of this car." With that said Worps sat on the hood and grabbed a windshield wiper. A couple of the guys joined him, while others sat on the trunk. Bulldog drove the mile and a half trip as the lone inside occupant of the vehicle. It was lunacy, but Worps' rarely did anything normal.

In late November, the city began a roadwork project in the alley parking area behind the Bluff Street house. Worps & Bulldog parked their cars out front but had to move them regularly to avoid getting parking tickets. Bulldog was tenacious about avoiding tickets, but Worps was a little more careless. He began to pile them up on the floor of his bedroom. After practice one day he noticed his car was nowhere to be seen.

"Do you think it was stolen or towed?" Worps asked feeling relieved. Since his car was missing, he assumed he was no longer responsible for all the parking tickets.

The big red Boat, with Gibby wearing the safety helmet, at the helm.

November 29th & 30th, 1980:

Saints 17, Waterloo 3 (away)

Saints 9, Bloomington 2 (home)

"Thomas' 4 goals, defense helps Saints smash Stars" -Telegraph Herald

It was Jack's first return to Waterloo. The rumor back in Waterloo was that Black Hawk fans were not as mad about Jack leaving as much as the fact that he took the five second year players with him. Jack decided he would rub a little salt into the wound. "Mel, Gibby. You two are starting on defense. Worps, Badger and Reegs on forward," Jack declared. The five former Black Hawks started the game and scored on the first shift. The Saints went on to win by a score of 17-3.

After trouncing the Black Hawks in Waterloo, the Saints beat up on the Bloomington Junior Stars at home. On this weekend the Saints outscored their opponents 26 to 5. It was a phenomenal margin and a night to celebrate. They all decided to meet up at the Walnut Tap after the game.

Walking home after the game, Bucky and Vogy found a bowling ball on the side of the road. Bucky decided to carry it a mile and half back to their apartment. When they got to the Walnut near their apartment, he looked up the hill towards their home, then back at the Walnut. Vogy knew what Bucky was thinking. He was pondering how good a beer would taste versus lugging the stupid bowling ball another couple blocks up the hill. Decision made, he sent the ball rolling down University Avenue. They watched it for a while but soon realized it wasn't going to stop. It was actually picking up speed as it progressed down the hill. With fear in their eyes and not wanting to see the

97

results, they ran inside for the cold refreshments just as they heard the loud thud of the ball coming to its final resting place. They never knew what stopped it. The next time they walked to the arena they saw no sign of the ball or any damage it may have caused.

The Walnut was the usual starting off point for a celebration night. A majority of the guys would then head up to the college bars looking for female companionship. Gibby and Worps stayed behind with Deano and Collins as closing time neared. The Walnut gave last call at ten minutes to one.

"I don't want to go home yet. We just got started," said Gibby.

Collins looked at Gibby and grinned. "Hop in the truck. We're going to East Dubuque. The bars stay open until four."

Gibby was apprehensive about going to the East Dubuque bars. He never heard good stories about going to those bars. "I'm not sure about that. Has anyone got some beer at home?" Gibby asked, trying to avoid the trip across the river.

"Come on Gibby, its not that bad. Are you hungry? They've got Coney dogs for a buck, I'll buy," said Collins.

Food was Gibby's weak spot so he agreed to go along. Worps decided to call it a night. They dropped him off on the way.

"I've heard some bad things about these places," said Gibby on the way over the bridge. He was still skeptical about stepping foot in what he called the "professional" bars of East Dubuque.

"Don't worry Gibby. If someone starts a fight, I've got a knife," said Deano with an awkward smile. Deano didn't carry a knife; he was just trying to get Gibby scared now that they had him captive in the truck. They took a left after getting off the bridge and parked the truck in a public parking spot across the street from the row of bars.

"We'll go to this first one here and get a couple beers before we get some food," said Collins pointing towards the closest bar.

As they were crossing the street, the doors to the bar flew open, and then a pair of bouncers threw a drunken patron face first onto the slushy curb. "Don't ever come back in here again!" they barked at the woman. That's right, it was an extremely drunk, slightly heavy-set woman in her late 20's that they threw onto the curb. She was not giving up without a fight. She got back up, staggered towards the door and threw a couple sloppy punches at the bouncers. Not impressed, they pushed her back to the ground violently. "We are warning you, don't step foot in here again!" With that proclamation they stepped back inside, letting the door slam behind them.

"Ahhh, maybe we'll go to the other one down the street," said Collins. Deano laughed. Gibby almost pissed his pants. He wanted to go back across the river fast. He was no longer hungry. In fact, he thought he was going to puke.

December 6th & 7th, 1980:

St. Paul 6, Saints 4 (home)

Saints 8, Waterloo 3 (away)

"Saints lose early margin, bow to St. Paul" -*Telegraph Herald*

Not every player came to Dubuque seeking a college scholarship. Some were there just to continue to play the game after high school, delaying the inevitable nine-to-five monotonous job they all knew they would be forced to endure soon enough in their young lives.

Worps had no intention of going to college. In the prior season Worps, Gibby and several other Waterloo Black Hawks took a trip to some Division II colleges in Minnesota. These trips did not impress Worps. He knew that he would have to find a real job to pay his grocery bills when the Saints season ended. He wanted to delay the real world as long as he could.

"Worps is from Vegas and never did anything normal," recalled Gibby. "I'm pretty sure Worps will never know what the real world is." Gibby tried to get Worps to play Division II hockey with him in Minnesota, but Worps wasn't interested in getting a degree.

Collins was also hoping to avoid the college route. He was hoping to move up through the minor league program similar to Barzee's playing career.

Others were looking at Division II or III schools to continue to play hockey while getting an education. They knew their own skill level and came to the realization early that there would be no scholarship waiting for them at the end of the season. Many hoped for a scholarship, but if none came, they would try

100

the "walk-on" method of making a team. To be successful as a walk-on, the coach had to know who you were, where you came from, and what kind of player you could be. Walk-on players rarely played as freshmen or sophomores. They could work their butts off for one or two years before they got to play in a single game.

The obvious players to be considered for a scholarship were the guys leading the team in goals and/or assists. College recruiters were looking for goal scorers with the natural scoring ability that Bulldog had. But they also looked for play making skills. Those that could "see the ice" better and passed the puck. Bulldog had that skill too. Then the recruiters looked for skating skills. This is where Grillo excelled. He was a strong natural skater.

It was no surprise when Bulldog and Grillo were asked to take a recruiting trip to Western Michigan University in early December. It was an all-expense paid trip to Kalamazoo for two days. They flew out of Dubuque on a Thursday and were expected back for the game on Saturday night against the St. Paul Vulcans.

After arriving in Kalamazoo they visited with the coaches who showed them around the campus, then they were able to watch a home game on Friday night. After the game they got to partake in the college party life, which earned them a decent hangover the next morning. Early on Saturday morning, they had separate meetings with the coaching staff.

"What do you think? Do you see yourself playing there next year?" Grillo asked Bulldog on the flight to Chicago.

"I'm pretty sure they think I'm too stupid to go to school there. They were not impressed with my high school GPA," replied Bulldog.

They did not talk much about it the rest of the way to Chicago, preferring instead to get in a nap before they had to rush through the airport to catch the connecting flight to Dubuque. Their itinerary said they would make it back to Dubuque three hours before the start of the game with St. Paul.

They landed in Chicago and got to the connecting gate quickly. "Ahhh, excuse me ma'am but the flight to Dubuque says cancelled. Is that some kind of mistake?" Grillo said to the airline attendant at the info desk.

"No, most of northern Illinois is locked down by fog. That flight won't be going out until tomorrow. I'm sorry." She said.

"See if you can find a bar. I'll call Jack and see what he wants us to do," Bulldog said. He figured they might as well get "lit-up" again if they were going to have to spend the night in Chicago.

"Jack, we're at O'Hare. We aren't going to make it back tonight. We're fogged in," Bulldog said.

"What? See if a bus is heading this way. I'll see if I can send someone over to pick you up!" Jack wailed over the phone. Jack did the distance/time ratio in his head and determined it would take more than 6 hours to get them back to Dubuque. They would miss the game.

Bulldog called Jack back and had to throw another quarter into the phone. "Son of a bitch, I can't afford to call him anymore," Bulldog whispered to himself. "What, ah, no Jack, I wasn't talking to you. We got bus tickets that should get us there at eight. That is the best option we had."

Jack determined that would get them into the arena halfway through the game. "Ok, but when you get here, you guys get dressed fast and be ready to play right away. You won't get a warm-up shift," said Jack.

"Gotcha, we'll be ready," said Bulldog. They skipped the bar and caught a cab to the bus station.

None of them realized that the fog was so thick that it affected the bus schedule. On the bus the guys felt like they were traveling at a snails pace. "We aren't going to make it, are we?" Bulldog said to Grillo.

"Not a chance. We should have stayed in Chicago and closed down the bar," replied Grillo.

At the start of the third period, Jack looked at his watch and wondered if they would make it at all. The Saints were down by a goal and Jack paced uneasily on the bench as play got underway.

The star recruits got to the arena in the third period with about 14 minutes remaining in the game. The Saints were losing 6-4. Bulldog and Grillo felt helpless as they walked up to the Plexiglas in front of the locker room and looked over towards Barzee. They assumed they didn't have enough time to put all their gear on and get on the ice.

Barzee motioned to them to get their butts out on the ice! The fans noticed the commotion and recognized who it was. They started a rousing cheer for the two tardy star players. Basking in the revelry they waved to the crowd then looked back towards a pissed off Barzee pointing towards the locker room. They came to their senses immediately and rushed into the locker room to get dressed.

"Scanny, go out there and fake an injury. Stall as long as you can, but don't make it too obvious," Jack said.

Scanny went out on the ice and flew up the rink looking for someone to hit. "This is kinda fun, maybe I'll wait 'till the end of the shift before I go down," Scanny thought. When he got tired enough, he ran into the closest opponent and went down. "I think it's broken," Scanny said after TD came out onto the ice to see what was wrong. TD tried to look concerned as he tended to the fake injury, but he couldn't hold back a laugh anytime Scanny said, "Oww, that

Inside The Locker Room

hurts." The ref never knew why the trainer was laughing at a guy with a potentially serious injury. The linesmen, Stoltzy and Waddy, knew what was going on.

The crowd roared as Scanny finally got to his feet, but it wasn't for Scanny. Bulldog and Grillo had just opened the gate to come out onto the ice at the same time, in full gear, ready to turn this game around. There was a little over ten minutes left in the game, and they were still down by two goals.

The cavalry had arrived to pull victory from the jaws of defeat...but they couldn't do it. The late arrivers were pretty much a non-factor. The game ended with the same score as when they arrived, a 6-4 loss.

Worps let them have it in the locker room after the game, "I thought you guys were big shots? You couldn't even score a single goal...pathetic losers."

December 10th, 1980:

Saints 7, Austin 4 (home)

"Big third period hands Saints 7-4 victory" *-Telegraph Herald*

He was nervous to be sitting on an animal this big. Bucky was dating a girl that was into the rodeo. He was trying to impress her with his riding skills and bravery by being the first to volunteer to ride the big bull. He gripped the leather handle with the palm of his left hand and pulled tightly, as if he could break it off but the handle wouldn't budge. It was designed that way. The bull was rather large, but it seemed very tame, at least for the moment.

With a solid look of determination on his face, Bucky put his right arm up in the air for balance and said, "Ok, I'm ready. Let him go!"

The bull started out slow without bucking or turning. There was no real threat of getting thrown off. With each passing fraction of a second, Bucky's confidence was growing. "Maybe I can do this," he thought. Just then the bull starting turning and twisting in an attempt to throw it's rider but Bucky held his balance and grip. Finally, the bull gave one big lunge combined with a turn. Bucky was sent flying over the top of the big bull, landing face first with a thud.

The thirty or forty witnesses to the incident groaned as he hit the ground. Bucky stood up, motioning to the crowd that he was OK. The patrons went back to drinking their beer, shooting pool or whatever else they were doing inside the bar.

This wasn't a real bull. It was a mechanical bull at Bucko's bar located near the Kennedy Mall. Bucko's was a favorite hangout for the players when they had nights off from their playing responsibilities

"You only lasted 2.6 seconds! I'm sure she's impressed with that," said Worps after he took of sip of his Old Style beer.

"Really? It seemed like much longer than that," Bucky looked at the clock. Sure enough it read 2.6 seconds. The bull's difficulty setting was at 5 on a scale of 1 to 10. Bucky shook his head in disgust and asked for another beer from the bartender.

The mechanical bull was a trend in a lot of bars in 1980 due to the popularity of the movie Urban Cowboy with John Travolta and Debra Winger. Most of the guys took a shot at the bull at some point during the season. Most of them had to get properly prepared by drinking enough beer to give them the courage, or more accurately, the stupidity to jump on that thing.

After several beers Gibby wanted to give it a try. He and Worps lifted weights throughout the summer. He assumed his strength combined with his shorter arm length would give him an advantage over Bucky.

"Put the setting at six," Gibby said confidently as he jumped onto the bull. The area around the bull was covered with a foot of vinyl covered foam padding, so he assumed he could not get injured. His plan was to close his eyes and hold as tight as possible.

"Ok, let 'em ride!" Gibby said as he closed his eyes and prepared for the onslaught. He lasted all of 1.2 seconds. Closing his eyes was a dumb idea. When he hit padding he still had his eyes closed and his arm extended. It hurt a lot. He thought he separated his shoulder. He played the rest of the season with constant pain in that shoulder but never told Jack or Doc Field how he got injured. He feared they would make Bucko's off limits.

They should have banned the players from Bucko's. Not just because of the bull riding but also because it was dangerous.

On another night one of the guys convinced a young lady to drive him home because he was too drunk to drive. At closing time they left the parking lot with her driving. On the way out of the parking lot they clipped a parked car. It made a loud thud and she stopped. Realizing that she was also too drunk to drive, he told her to keep going. If she stayed she would be in serious trouble. They left the scene, switching drivers a mile or two down the road.

The guys frequented Bucko's less as the season wore on. It made more sense to go to the Walnut because it was within walking distance and the beer was cheaper. For the guys who lived in the 11th Street apartments, the Walnut was in their backyard. Collins was a regular there. He would call down to have them prepare soup and other food for him. He knew the owners, Ron and Helen Weiner, on a first name basis.

"Hey Ronny, what's the game today?" Collins said wondering which college football teams were playing. It was the place Collins would go to watch TV. If you ever needed to get a hold of Collins, you would call the Walnut. If he wasn't there, they would know where to find him.

December 13th & 14th, 1980:

Green Bay 7, Saints 5 (away)

Saints 4, Bloomington 3 (away)

"Saints edge Stars in OT" -Telegraph Herald

"Clarence!" the guys cheered when Clarence got on the bus. Weekend road games away were the worst. Too many long hours on the bus made it miserable. They rarely had two games in the same town on a weekend series. In between games, they had to take another multi-hour bus ride, and then get off the bus with the expectation of playing at peak performance. At least they had Clarence, the "good-guy" bus driver for this trip.

A big win on the road in Green Bay had the guys in good spirits. They ate supper together after the game then headed to the hotel. Jack had to put four players in each room because the Fighting Saints organization was limited on funds. Deano, Collins, Scanny and Jask roomed together. After the long bus ride and the big win they still had a lot of energy to release.

In the hotel room Jask produced a Nerf basketball and a pair of hoops. In the beginning of the season, Jask participated in an indoor football game at the Bluff Street house. This time it was full contact basketball in a small hotel room.

They set up a mini basketball court with the hoops suction cupped to the walls above each bed. The beds served as the court so it would be quiet and safe. They just had to make sure they didn't put their heads through the ceiling when they jumped around on the court.

The game went smoothly until they started doing flying slam-dunks. With the game tied Deano went for a slam-dunk over the top of Scanny. With every bit of resistance he could muster, Scanny grabbed Deano around the waist as he flew overhead, throwing him onto the bed. They heard a loud crack when they landed in a heap, piled up between the bed and the wall. They lay there laughing for a moment before realizing what happened. Two legs broke off, leaving the bed tilting at a precarious angle.

All four of them sat on the good bed surveying the situation for several minutes. "That looks bad," said Scanny.

"I've got an idea," Collins said. He looked under the broken bed at the two remaining intact legs, and then he broke them off one at a time.

"What are you doing?" Scanny yelled as Collins finished the job.

Collins then straightened up the bed sheets and stepped back to admire his work. "There. Now it's even," he declared.

"When Jack comes in at bed-check time, he's gonna notice that one bed is taller than the other," Jask said.

Collins stood in the middle of the room pondering this for a moment. "Hmmm, You're right. Get up," he said. Then he broke off the four legs on the good bed to make them all look even. "There. Looks good to me," Collins said satisfied with his work. Scanny watched in astonishment.

"What are we gonna do with the broken legs?" Jask said. Deano grabbed the broken legs, put them in the shower and covered them with a towel. Mission accomplished.

Jack knocked on the door several minutes later and entered the room. "You guys got any injuries I need to know about," he asked.

"Nope, we're all good. Just watching TV and getting ready to go to bed," said Jask. Scanny was pretending to read a book, trying desperately not to appear nervous. Sweat was still beading on his forehead from the basketball game in addition to being nervous. Barzee left without noticing the shorter beds. Scanny let out a sigh of relief as the door closed behind Jack. The four scoundrels slept comfortably that night on broken beds.

The next day they made the trip to Bloomington, Minnesota, defeating the Junior Stars in overtime. The two big road wins had them in celebration mode. Jack and Clarence allowed them to get some beer for the bus ride home. Jack would've never allowed the beer stop if he knew about the hotel beds. The four bed-breakers kept their mouths shut, never telling the other players about the results of the hotel basketball game.

While the guys were buying beer for the way home, Jask and Reegs hooked the bus speakers to a battery powered car stereo they brought with them. The bad-guy driver never let Jask and Reegs bring the car battery on the bus, but Clarence didn't mind. They played music for a while and then started singing their own songs. The guys sang their own version of "In The Good Old Summertime." This song was a regular event on the bus rides.

In the good ol' wintertime, in the good ol' wintertime,

Skating on Green Bay ice, on a forward line.

We shoot the puck,

We score a goal,

And that's a really good time.

We're out to win the USHL in the good ol' wintertime.

After the songs and music settled down, they gathered in small groups, some played cards and drank beer. They talked about the game and played backgammon. They played more backgammon. Worps was an expert backgammon player. He had his own professional board he brought along on road trips. Reegs enjoyed beating Worps with off-the-wall moves. "That's not even smart," Worps said.

"Yah, but I beat you, didn't I" replied Reegs.

"Like, one time out of five," said Worps.

"Doesn't matter, I won!" declared Reegs, and with that he ended the match. Worps shook his head in disgust.

Nordsy did his homework; on occasion he would ask Collins for help. After a couple hours the bus grew quiet as players started to nod off. For some players sleeping on the bus was easy. They closed their eyes and they were out cold. For others there would be no sleep. No matter how hard they tried, they could not get comfortable enough to sleep.

The team didn't have the nice sleeper buses they have nowadays. The skinny guys (Chris Guy and Jask) would crawl up into the overhead luggage area to spread out. The larger ones (Gibby and Bucky) tried to fit under the seats. Some guys laid out in the aisles but they usually got wet from melting snow. These were the only places to stretch out. It didn't help much because people would step on them while heading to the bathroom in the back of the bus.

When the bus got near Durango the curves and turns made the cans roll around waking up the players. It was the perfect alarm clock telling the players it was time to get ready to go home.

Two weeks later Jack received a bill from the hotel in Green Bay. The only things listed on the bill were line items for Bed Frame 1 and Bed Frame 2.

December 17th, 1980:

Saints 10, Des Moines 4 (home)

"Saints clobber Des Moines" -Telegraph Herald

It was the perfect opportunity for Mel. The guy came up the ice with his head down. Mel knew when a guy was vulnerable to the big hit. When a guy is focusing too much on the puck, Mel would step up and clobber him.

Mel never paid much attention to the puck except that it made an opposing player fair game to be crushed. If they had the puck, they were targets. Sometimes it didn't matter if they had the puck, he would crush them anyway, as long as the puck was nearby.

Mel lined up the player coming across the red line and flattened him. The Buccaneer players took exception to the hit. One of them threw off his gloves and started throwing punches. It was exactly what Mel wanted. The two exchanged punches until Mel connected on one that buckled the Buccaneers knees. As he went to the ice, Stoltzy and Waddy jumped in to break the fight. Another Buccaneer jumped into the melee and threw a punch at Mel. He tried it to connect with a haymaker that would knock Mel out. It had the completely opposite effect. It made Mel mad, crazy mad.

The Buccaneer sensed what was coming and tried to escape into the safety of his player's bench. Surely Mel would not be crazy enough to follow him in there, would he? Mel skated into the Buccaneer bench, grabbed the guy by the jersey and pulled him back out onto the ice. He proceeded to beat him senseless while fending off the linesmen. It was Mel's second and final fight of the evening. He was ejected from the game.

There were plenty of fights in this game. Earlier Worps fought one of the Buccaneer goons in a battle that resorted to hair pulling and eye gouging. Even Fallon got into a good brawl. Once again the linesmen had to protect the Buccaneer player from a crazed Saint. Fallon wouldn't stop when the linesmen came into break it up. His fight earned him 9 minutes in penalties.

Whenever the Saints played Des Moines, there would be multiple fights. It was always a battle. The Buccaneers were always looking for a fight, but they bit off more than they could chew with Mel.

Battleship Bailey was arguably the toughest fighter in the history of the USHL. Mel was built like an NFL linebacker and played hockey like one too. He never missed an opportunity to step up from his defensive position to take out an opposing player. He loved to hear the cheers of the crowd when he connected on a good hit. He especially liked the roar of the crowd when he was fighting.

The only time Mel got hurt in a fight was in the previous season. During a bench-clearing brawl, two guys teamed up on him. One guy hit Mel in the chin with his stick, splitting his chin wide open. His face was a mess for several weeks.

The most anyone could hope for in a fair fight with Mel was a draw. There were a few players on every team that would challenge Mel on a regular basis. If his opponents managed to land a few punches, none seemed to hurt Mel. On the other hand, when Mel connected with a punch, the guy would fall just in time to avoid the next punch headed towards his face. If the guy was lucky, the linesmen would break up the fight early enough to save him from a more brutal beating.

Off the ice Mel Bailey was one of the quietest guys on the team. He was very shy, keeping to himself most of the time.

At Christmas break Gibby begged Mel to give him a ride back to the cities. He was afraid the Boat's brakes would fail again and he would be stranded. At the beginning of the season, Mel brought a big heavy-bag down in the passenger seat of his car. He wanted to use it for workouts. Unfortunately, there was nowhere to hang it up at the Bluff Street house so he decided to bring it back home at the Christmas break. The heavy-bag would take up the whole front passenger seat of his Datsun 280Z. Mel was proud of that car. It was a nice car but had no back seat for storage. It was the complete opposite of Gibby's Boat.

"Come on Mel, I promise to bring the heavy bag home in my car after the season and personally deliver it to your door," Gibby pleaded.

"Nope, there's no room," was Mel's reply.

After Mel left for the cities alone with his heavy-bag, Worp's changed Mel's nickname to "Selfish Mel." The nickname stuck with him for weeks. Worps soon tired of that name and just called him "Mud."

During the season Mel never responded to Worp's name calling. He would shrug it off like it was not important. It was hard to understand their relationship. Worps and Mel had spent most of the last three years together, a year of high school then two USHL seasons on the same team. They got along ok, but Worps ridiculed Mel relentlessly.

Mel did have one person of which he was very close. He had a girlfriend back in Rosemount, Minnesota, that he cherished. Mel's girlfriend gave him a pair of dress shoes that were too small for his feet. He didn't have the heart to tell her. To avoid conflict he would bring two pairs of shoes whenever the team would travel to the Twin Cities for games. He wore the tight shoes to and from the game when he met with his girlfriend, then he would immediately take them off and put on a more comfortable pair when he got on the bus.

This is the same guy that would pulverize opponent's faces with both fists, kick small kittens and push old ladies down escalators. Ok, he never did the last two, but there are people that believe he was mean enough to do them all. Off the ice he was a gentleman and stayed out of the limelight. On the ice, he was a beast. His teammates, including Worps, appreciated the fact that he was on their side whenever the going got rough.

December 19th, & 20th, 1980:

Des Moines 9, Saints 7 (away)

Saints 10, Sioux City 4 (away)

"Saints split two matches" -Telegraph Herald

TD was unable to make the road trip because of his work schedule. Jim Denman volunteered to act as the team trainer even though he had virtually no experience or training in that capacity.

The Saints lost to the Buccaneers the night before in typical Saints-Buccaneers fashion, penalties and fights. The Saints received ten penalties in the third period alone, the Buccaneers only three. This sealed the game for the Buc's.

Now it was on to Sioux City and hopefully a milder game in which the Saints could concentrate on putting pucks in the net. Jim was on the bus thinking how lucky he was last night in Des Moines. He only had to fill a few ice bags to fulfill his duties as acting athletic trainer. For the most part he helped carry equipment and ran errands for Jack. "This game should be easier," he thought.

It was Jim's first trip to the hockey arena in Sioux City. It didn't take him long to realize that all the stories he heard about it being a "shit-hole" were true. He looked at the bench that went perpendicular to the ice. He knew he would not be able to watch the game. Standing at the back of the bench, he made sure the water bottles were full and handed out sticks if a player needed a replacement.

Early in the second period the game was notched at two apiece when Collins put in the go-ahead goal with an assist from Deano. The next shift on the ice, Deano carried the puck into the attacking zone skirting a Musketeer defender we'll call the Kamikaze. The Kamikaze swung at the puck with his stick. Deano defended the gesture with his body. That was the normal procedure. But this time the Kamikaze swung too high. He hit Deano in the chin leaving a deep gash, dropping him to the ice.

Jim Denman was summoned from the back of the bench to attend to Deano's wound. He went out onto the ice with a towel but when he saw the gash, he was mortified. He escorted Deano back to the bench to study the wound more carefully.

"Jack, this is gonna require stitches. I don't know what to do?" Jim yelled up to Jack at the front of the bench.

Jack was busy now, as the game was getting tense. The Musketeers were putting on pressure. Jack didn't have time to deal with Jim's problems.

"Just tape him up with some strips, I need him out on the ice, NOW!" was Jack's response.

"What strips, I don't know what..." Jim replied back in a panic.

"Thin Band-Aids, in the med-kit," Jack said cutting him off.

"What the hell are thin Band-Aids?" Jim mumbled to himself as he rummaged through the first-aid kit. It was the first time he opened it.

"They're the little white ones," Deano's voice was muffled by the towel over his mouth, but Jim still understood what he said.

Jim put six Steri-Strips, alias thin Band-Aids, on Deano's chin. After a few moments, he was skeptical they would hold. He wasn't even sure he put them on correctly. "Jack, I don't think he should go out there," Jim advised.

117

Jack looked at Deano, "You want a shot at the Kamikaze?" Deano nodded affirmatively.

Back on the ice, Deano got his chance to even the score. Before he could even drop his gloves, the Kamikaze slapped him across the ear rupturing his eardrum. Now Deano was really pissed and punched him in the face with his right hand. His right hand still had a plaster cast on it from the separated thumb earlier in the season. The Kamikaze's face was a mess, just like Deano's. This time however, it was the Kamikaze that was skated off with a towel.

After serving his penalty, Deano returned to the ice. The ruptured eardrum was affecting his balance. He was stumbling and appeared off kilter. Thinking it was from the messed up chin, Jim protested again to Jack. He thought a professional trainer, or anyone that knew something about thin Band-Aids should attend to Deano. Bloodied and off balance, Deano finished the game.

The Saints beat Sioux City 10-4 and loaded the bus for the red-eye trip back to Dubuque. Before the bus headed out of Sioux City, Jim protested to Jack one more time. "Jack, we need to stop at the hospital to get Deano stitched up," Jim said.

"We don't have time. We gotta get on the road. Deano can go see Doc Field tomorrow," Jack replied.

Deano never went to see Doc Field. He felt comfortable that Jim's thin Band-Aids would do the job. He also had his girlfriend, Christy, to take care of him. The next day Deano slept in and waited for Christy to get off work. She told him he needed to go to the hospital for stitches, but he never took the time. The long scar on Deano's chin is clearly visible today.

December 28th, 1980:

Saints 9, Sioux City 3 (home)

"Capacity crowd watches Saints drub Sioux City" -Telegraph Herald

On New Year's Eve there was a capacity crowd at the house on Bluff Street. The gathering was a big party for the players and invited guests. It was planned only a few days in advance.

"What do you think about having a kegger party here on New Year's Eve?" Grillo asked the guys sitting around the slanted TV.

"That would cost money," said Bulldog. The guys rarely did anything that cost money if it wasn't a necessity. Necessities were food, rent and supplies like toothpaste and soap. The latter usually arrived in care packages from home. Beer might have been considered a necessity. Buying it in that quantity was considered extravagant, even if they might actually make money in the long run. They calculated that two 16-gallon kegs would cost them about $72, plus deposit and cups. Grillo agreed to put up a majority of the money if everyone pitched in.

"What about my tapper fridge? We gotta do 8-gallon kegs. It has the tap built in and it will save us money on the deposit," said Gibby trying to sell idea to his teammates. 16-gallon kegs wouldn't fit in the tapper fridge's small frame.

Worps said, "Wait a second. Didn't you tell me that tapper only works with Schmidt beer?" It was true; it only worked with Schmidt kegs so the guys dismissed Gibby's argument.

119

Gibby didn't give in. "It'll keep the beer cold for weeks if we don't drink it all," he argued. A compromise was reached where they would get one 8 gallon keg of Schmidt, and one 16 gallon keg of Old Style. It saved them about twenty dollars. With this solution they would only have to sell about 30 cups at $2 each to break even.

Worps didn't like the idea "If we run out of beer, Gibby...it's on your head"

That night they drubbed Sioux City 9-3 in front of a huge sellout crowd. Hundreds of fans turned away at the gate. It was the first capacity crowd of the season. Betty Weiland estimated she turned away more than 400 people at the entrance. She felt really bad that she had to tell people they couldn't get in to see the game.

The next day, the Bluff Street house was getting cleaned up for the New Year's bash. Actually, it was more organizing than it was cleaning; they just moved everything that wasn't nailed down into the basement.

They had a nice Christmas tree, but nobody really knew how it got there. The rumor was that someone went out into the woods and cut it down; but there were no woods nearby and none of the cars had pine needles in them, so it remained a mystery. There were two other rumors floated around. One was that the neighbor ladies, Laurie, Shelly and Julie bought it for the guys. The other was that Worps walked down the street until he found a suitable tree in someone's yard. The first is more plausible because they didn't have a saw. Regardless, the tree was decorated with a few bulbs, trinkets and a few lights that they found in the basement. Worps did most of the decorating because he was the only player on the team that didn't go home during the four day Christmas break.

They invited friends and fans by word of mouth. Grillo was worried Jack would find out and cancel the whole party. Badger didn't think Jack would care if they didn't let it get out of hand.

The party was well attended and everything remained calm until late in the night. Grillo and Carlson went outside and returned with two bus stop signs. The signs stood about six feet tall if you count the concrete part they pulled out of the ground.

"They came out pretty easy," said Grillo. "We just wiggled them a little bit and they popped right out."

"What in the heck are those for?" asked Worps.

"Jousting," replied Grillo.

Bulldog and Grillo faced off against each other in the first jousting match. Dirt flew in all directions when the two swords clashed. What could possibly get out of hand with two 19-year-old juveniles jousting with bus stop signs?

The next day the guys dragged themselves out of their rooms with severe hangovers. There was puke on all three floors. In the living room there were two bent up bus signs and dirt strewn everywhere.

The guys blamed the illness on Gibbys' beer fridge. The tap lines hadn't been used in so long that it had bacteria in it that made them all sick. That was the theory they came up with. No one considered the possibility that they just drank too much. Either way they had a lot of real cleaning to do this time. On the bright side, they broke even financially. There was also a good portion of cold beer in Gibby's fridge. Unfortunately, no one was willing to drink it because of the bacteria scare. Eventually the beer went stale, the keg was returned for the deposit and the tapper fridge went back to being a milk cooler.

January 3rd & 4th, 1981:

Saints 7, Bloomington 1 (home)

Saints 5, Waterloo 1 (away)

"CBS takes America's pulse in Dubuque" -*Telegraph Herald*

Jack Barzee was back in Waterloo for the third time this season. Up to this point he was too busy to sit back and take stock in his professional choices. Starting out the New Year in Waterloo was kind of ironic for him. His wife, Kathy, was finally warming up to the transition to the new city. Their kids were fully adjusted as well. He was pretty sure he made the right choice, but he still had doubts in the back of his mind.

He stood behind the player's bench at the old McElroy Auditorium in Waterloo, pondering all this as the starting lineups were being announced. A crackling noise startled him back to the present as the National Anthem began to play. The PA system stopped working. For several moments there was nothing but silence.

"Oh say can you see, by the dawn's early light..." a section of the crowd began singing the National Anthem without any music or words to guide them.

Barzee thought, "That's not too bad." He turned around to see where the singing was coming from. It was coming from the Dubuque fan section. All the fans that came over in cars, trucks and vans from Dubuque, a hundred or more crazy loyal fans from Dubuque, sang the entire National Anthem. A smattering of Waterloo fans joined in the middle of the song.

Jack turned back around with a grin on his face. "These Dubuque fans really are amazing people," he thought. They were new to the game of hockey, but they loved it. There was a passion there that Jack wasn't able to produce in Waterloo.

The previous home game in Dubuque was another sellout crowd. Hundreds of fans were willing to pay for standing room only tickets. That kind of passion led to pre-game parties at bars and restaurants, tailgating in parking lots, and dressing up in costumes. The Blues Brothers showed up for several games, and there was even an Elvis sighting in the crowd. The town was smitten with the game of hockey and the winning ways of the Saints.

It was reciprocal. The players were amazed by the kindness and passion of the fans. Regular meals in family homes were the norm. That didn't happen in Waterloo the year before. The hockey fans in Dubuque were different from other cities in the league. The players couldn't understand why they were all so nice. "What do they see in us that makes them think we're special? We certainly don't deserve it," said Gibby.

"Obviously they don't know what kind of pathetic losers we really are," replied Worps.

The fans generosity wasn't an act because they never wanted anything in return for their kindness. The only real explanation is that vast majority of Dubuque people are inherently good, caring and passionate people.

Many of the players permanently bonded with families in the community: Bucky with the Martell's, Gibby with the Baxter's, Fallon with the Denman's, Badger with the Haas's, Worps with the Runde's, and many others. Even John DiNapoli, who was in Dubuque only four months, sends a Christmas card back once a year.

Later in January CBS filmed the Sunday Morning Show in Dubuque. CBS wanted to get the "Pulse" of the nation from Dubuque, Iowa. They wanted to know how people in Dubuque felt about the Iran hostages being released, about the high gas prices, about the high interest rates, and all other things they could complain about.

The film crew went to the Five Flags and filmed inside the locker room before a game. Then they filmed the fans during the game. On the show they called hockey in Dubuque a "distraction from the world's problems." Hockey in Dubuque was not a distraction; it was a passion.

Tom Hartjehausen, eighteen in 1981, missed only 2 home games in the history of the Saints at the Five Flags Center. Richard Lehnhardt traveled with friends on work nights to road games. Joe Baxter, Bill Hoerstman, and Chuck Haas were the core of a large group of men that made the games a family event. These hard working people had a strong sense of family. They were looking for a good time for young and old, male and female, to celebrate the games together. These are some of the many examples of the passion for hockey in Dubuque.

CBS chose Dubuque to take the "Pulse of America." However, they should have chosen some other city if they wanted the story to fit their preconceived notion of chronic complainers. Hockey in Dubuque was not a distraction and the people were not complainers.

Jack knew that Dubuque was a special place, with special people. The people of Dubuque have always taken great pride in their city, now they had a new team to call their own. After the Dubuque fan section finished singing the National Anthem Jack Barzee had no regrets. He felt blessed to be able to call Dubuque his new home.

January 10th, 1981:

Saints 10, Waterloo 3 (home)

"Mike Fallon: a tough life on ice" -*The Gleaner, Wahlert HS*

Just after 10AM the two high school seniors rolled into the Wahlert parking lot in Fallon's truck. Fallon passed by all the open spaces and stopped near the front entrance of the school.

"Are you not going in?" asked Nordsy. The regular weekday schedule for Fallon and Nordsy was hockey practice from 8 to 9:30 a.m., and then classes from 10 a.m. to 3 p.m. Fallon usually worked at Oak Ridge Sports for three or four hours in the evening and Nordsy studied.

Fallon thought about not replying at all to Nordsy's question but after a few moments he just said, "No."

This was the new procedure. Fallon would drive them to school but rarely attend classes. Nordsy was worried that Fallon would drop out. He knew that Fallon was not motivated to go to class.

"You ok?" asked Nordsy. Fallon nodded. Nordsy got out of the truck and headed in without looking back.

During the summer Jack made arrangements for any high school aged players that made the team to attend Wahlert Catholic High School. The administrators at Wahlert allowed the players to miss classes for practices and games that overlapped with school, as long as they completed assignments. Special arrangements were also made for the players to pick up homework in advance of road games. "Wahlert was very generous in working with our schedule," recalled Nordsy. Nordsy loved his time at Wahlert; the classes were fascinating and the students were accepting and friendly. At the beginning of the season, Fallon felt the same way; but soon he began skipping school. It may have been because he didn't feel challenged or perhaps because he grew tired of the busy hockey/school/work schedule. He never told Nordsy or any of his teammates.

On this day, like he had been doing for several weeks, Fallon decided he had more important things to do than go to class. After dropping off Nordsy at school, he drove his truck out into the country to watch some farm animals. Later he stopped by the Bluff Street house and watched soaps with Worps and Grillo. After an hour he got back in his truck and headed to work.

"What you got going on tonight?" Jim Denman asked as the customers thinned out and it came close to closing time.

"I've got some studying to do. I might go to the library," said Fallon.

At the Denman house Fallon skipped supper and drove away immediately after they got home. He made his way downtown parking on Bluff Street, but he wasn't stopping into see the guys. He was picking up Julie to go to a movie. Julie Avery was one of the three young ladies that let the guys watch soaps on their TV. She had dark hair, puppy dog eyes, full lips and a beautiful smile.

Julie and Fallon met for the first time a little over a week ago at the New Years Eve bash. They were immediately drawn to each other. While most of the others were partying and jousting with bus stop signs, Fallon and Julie talked their way into the New Year. They began dating regularly.

Back at the Denman house, Tony and Nordsy were watching TV in the family room, as Jim sat down in the recliner. Nordsy was living with the Doug Jass family but was spending a lot of his time at the Denman house with Fallon and Tony Denman.

"How's school going?" Jim asked Nordsy.

"Good, I guess. I'm surprised I'm not falling behind," Nordsy replied.

"Yah, Mike sure is spending a lot of time studying at the library," said Jim referring to Fallon.

"Yah, sure he is," Nordsy thought sarcastically but didn't say it out loud. "He might be studying, but he's not at the library; and the subject is not Trigonometry, it's Julie Avery."

Fallon used the library excuse regularly to get out of work early or to get out of the house without being asked questions. Jim and Ginny Denman were impressed that Fallon spent so much time "studying" at the library. They didn't know Fallon had a girlfriend until after the season ended. Fallon made it through high school without failing. How he did it remains a mystery.

January 11th, 1981:

University of Wisconsin 8, Saints 1 (home exhibition game)

"Saints get taste of own medicine, 8-1" -Telegraph Herald

They were all in the locker room talking about the upcoming game. It was a meaningless game, not even on the schedule, but it was a big test for the players. The Saints were stacking up wins and scoring goals in record fashion. It was close to mid-season, and it seemed like they could coast to the USHL title.

For some strange reason, Jack scheduled a home exhibition game against the University of Wisconsin, Junior Varsity. That's right, the JV! There was a lot of talk in town about this upcoming exhibition game. They questioned why the Saints were going to play a "JV" team. To the fans in Dubuque, it seemed like the Saints were very tough to beat, especially on home ice.

The fans were incredulous, "Why aren't we playing the Varsity?" Even a few of the city's prominent leaders wanted a shot at the Wisconsin Varsity squad. Not Doc Field. Doctor David Field was a giant in Dubuque, not just in his size. The players were impressed with his resume. He was born in Toronto, Alberta, and played hockey at the University of Toronto. He later played for the Kingston Aces, a precursor to the Canadian Olympic team. He moved to Dubuque after completing his education. Some said he broke so many bones in his playing career that he felt obliged to repent of his hockey sins by becoming an orthopedic surgeon. Earlier in the season he had the players over to his house and showed them his old hockey scrapbook. One piece caught the attention and awe of the players. It was an old Toronto newspaper article with a photo of him holding a player by the face with one hand; the other hand was cocked back seemingly ready to throw a devastating punch.

Doc Field was an original investor in the Fighting Saints organization. He knew a lot about the game of hockey. The former hockey tough guy, turned low-key gentleman, knew that the University of Wisconsin was a nationally ranked Division I team; one of the top 4 in the country at the time. "This would be "gut-check" time for the boys," he thought to himself; he smiled inside at all the controversy.

"Really, they want us to play the Varsity?" said Gibby.

"Apparently, they think we're good," Worps responded in his typical self-deprecating sarcastic fashion. Worps has a way of insulting people, without really insulting them, or vice versa. Either way Worps was always insulting. He made you laugh when he insulted you, so you couldn't really get mad at him. And he insulted himself, regularly.

"We'll kick their ass," said Collins with his trademark grin. Collins didn't really have a trademark on his grin but he should have. Nobody was sure if he was talking about the JV or the Varsity. It didn't matter because Collins was making a statement, even if it sounded crazy. Collins didn't make statements like that very often. Grillo was uneasy as he watched Collins whisper those words again.

"Don't worry Jimmy, he sleeps with that grin on," Deano said with his own devilish smile.

It's true. The famous Brian Collins grin was worn 24/7/365, and almost four decades later it's still there. It's the type of grin that if you didn't know him you would think he was bat-shit crazy. Collins is extremely even-keeled. He never gets rattled. He could be scoring goals or getting "run" by one of the opposing team's goons, but his demeanor and his trademark grin would stay the same through it all. The smart teammates didn't play poker with Collins on the bus. And the ones that did only played because those bus rides were so boring they would set aside money they could donate to Collins. He is sly like a fox and possessed all the skills of a master tradesman, including the determination to get any job done. He just never talked about it much. In fact, he didn't do much talking at all. Which is why Grillo was uneasy with his comments.

"I think he might just beat 'em by himself," Deano told Grillo. Then he laughed with his spooky laugh "he, he, heee." That didn't make Grillo feel any better about the situation. He knew this would be a very tough game. Grillo was hoping to show case his solid skating skills to prove he could play at the Division I level. He just wanted his teammates to take it seriously...and pass him the puck!

Deano was toying with Grillo. Deano was playing the best hockey of his career and he had every reason to be confident. Deano was one of the three members of the "Bulldog" line. The Bulldog line consisted of Collins on right wing, Deano on the left, and Bulldog at center.

With his hulking body Deano played a rough style of hockey. Moving Deano out of the front of the net was a daunting task, so most opposing players didn't even try. That is where Deano got most of his goals, picking up garbage for Bulldog and Collins. Deano is very similar to Collins in his demeanor, even-keeled and laid back. These guys rarely got angry on the ice, no matter what happened. And neither of them were bat-shit crazy. Which was too bad, because they could have used a little "crazy" when they played the Badgers..."JV."

The first period was a fast paced affair with back and forth action. The Saints were not outclassed. In fact, they had the edge in shots, but they couldn't get the puck past Wisconsin goalie Marc Behrend. Jask gave up one goal.

In the second period Wisconsin got six goals in eight minutes. The game was essentially over at that point, but the Saints never gave up. More than anything they wanted to score a goal on this goalie who was incredibly efficient at stopping the puck.

It was Collins, of course, who finally tallied for the Saints. It was a rocket of a wrist shot from the just inside the blue line that Collins pegged for the upper corner. Inside the locker room after the game, Collins sat in his corner with his regular grin, satisfied that he finally scored on that goalie.

The Saints took this game as seriously as any other game. Mel stood them up at the blue line but they were able to pass it by him. Gibby checked opposing shoulder pads with his face and was rewarded with a black eye and a bruised ego. The forwards were able to skate and pass freely, but Behrend was not letting anything get by him. The Collins goal with a little more than three minutes left in the game was the only Saints tally. The final score was 8-1.

There was no longer any talk of playing the varsity. However, it could be argued that they actually did play the varsity. Several varsity players were moved down to play in the game, including their starting goalie Marc Behrend. Ironically, less than two months after playing the Saints, Marc Behrend would lead the University of Wisconsin varsity team to the Division I National Championship as the tournament MVP. Regardless, the "JV" game was soon forgotten and the focus shifted back to softer USHL opponents.

Toronto newspaper photo of Doc Field (#5).
(photo courtesy of Doc Field)

January 17ᵗʰ & 18ᵗʰ, 1981:

Saints 7, Green Bay 6 (home)

Saints 2, Green Bay 1 (away)

"Saints edge Bobcats" -*Telegraph Herald*

Jack was already waiting at the Dubuque Regional Airport when the flight from Chicago touched down and taxied to a stop. An aircraft tug pushed the stairs into place and backed away, several seconds later passengers began de-boarding. John DiNapoli was the last passenger off the plane. He paused at the top of the steps in an attempt to see who might be waiting for him but all the people were inside where it was warm. Jack immediately knew which of the passengers was DiNapoli. He was the one wearing a full-length fur jacket and sporting what looked like a Fu-Man-Chu mustache.

"Oh boy," Jack thought to himself. He hoped it was not a mistake to bring in a player this late in the season. "I don't care what kind of weirdo he is, as long as he's good."

John DiNapoli was good and he came highly recommended. He was in his second year as a walk-on at the University of New Hampshire, a ranked Division I team. In his first year he played in twenty-five of the Wildcats twenty-eight games, notching one goal and three assists. After an illness that required him to miss two weeks of practice he couldn't get back in the lineup.

DiNapoli called his uncle who was a referee in the ECAC. His uncle said he knew a guy in Iowa that would give him a fair chance to play. After a several phone calls, Jack agreed to give him a one-week tryout, if he could make his own way to Dubuque.

Back at the airport Jack introduced himself. They loaded his gear in the car and headed to the Five Flags Center. Jack took DiNapoli into the locker room and told him to unpack his hockey gear in the corner and then he left to do some office work.

The guys heard rumors that Jack was bringing in some hotshot from New Hampshire. Most of the guys did not like the idea at the time. The new guy would cut into ice time, and they were already winning, so what would be the point?

Worps was ambivalent; he liked guys from the east coast. They usually had a strong accent and a quirky personality, both of which gave him lots of ammunition for insults. Of the current east coast players on the team, only Bucky had the typical New England accent. Worps would give him grief, and Bucky would give it right back. Fallon also had a strong New York accent. However, he didn't talk much so Worps gave him a break. The other two players from the east coast, Vogy and Scanny, could pass as mid-westerners.

DiNapoli was unpacking when Scanny came into the locker room by himself. Without hesitation Scanny said, "So you're the guy they got to replace me? I'm Glenn Scanlan, nice to meet you." He firmly shook his hand and then he left.

John DiNapoli (DiNap) stood five-feet ten inches tall, and weighed 180 lbs. He could play defense or forward. It didn't take long for the guys to know that DiNap would be a good addition to the team. The kid from Concord, New Hampshire could skate like the wind and had a stinging wrist shot.

After DiNap moved into the house on Bluff Street, Worps found out that he was actually a normal guy. Nothing he did gave him ammunition; but of course, that never stopped Worps...he was an equal opportunity annoyer. DiNap was a likable guy with an outgoing energetic personality and a charming smile. He quickly became one of the regular guys. DiNap even injured his groin after getting thrown from Bucko's bull.

DiNap made a big impact on the team. Off the ice he helped the guys with social norms. "Wait a second," he said "you can't go to someone's house and eat their food without giving a gift. If we all pitch in fifty cents or a buck we can get a decent bottle of wine." Dinap was aghast that these players were invited to eat at family homes and they never brought a gift. Most of these guys lacked common social skills. DiNap was educating them. It took some getting used to, but the guy with the fur jacket was right.

After walking into the kitchen and seeing the mess of dishes, DiNap began doing dishes. That was unheard of. The guys never cleaned dishes unless it was mealtime; then they only did the dishes they needed for that meal, nothing more. After a week of doing dishes and getting no help, DiNap told everyone that they needed take their own dishes back to their rooms. If they wanted to live in a "pigs sty" they could do it in their own room, not in the kitchen. Finally he got some cooperation.

On the ice DiNap added a scoring and passing punch that helped strengthen everyone on the team: everyone except Scanny. Scanny took the arrival of DiNap as sign for him to move on.

"Jack, I think you should trade me back to Waterloo," Scanny said to Jack in a private meeting he requested soon after DiNapoli arrived. As a coach, Jack wanted to give everyone a chance to play and develop. It was his job not just to win games and sell tickets, but also to develop players. Jack took that responsibility seriously, so he agreed to let Scanny go. Two days later, Scanny packed up his Datsun B210 and headed west to become a Black Hawk. The guys were not happy but they understood. Many of them had been in similar situations; it was better for Scanny to move on.

135

January 21st & 24th, 1981:

Saints 11, Des Moines 1 (home)
Saints 6, Des Moines 3 (away)

"Saints win ninth straight" -Telegraph Herald

They hated playing the Buccaneers. Every game this season against Des Moines has been a penalty followed by a fight and vice-versa. It was the only way the Buccaneers could beat the Saints. Going into Des Moines the players knew when they returned their jerseys would smell like beer. Apparently Des Moines fans didn't like the beer they sold at the arena, because it always ended up getting poured on the Saints.

The coach of the Buccaneers was Crazy Ivan Prediger. Crazy Ivan was a huge barrel chested man with long thin mustache and no neck; his big square head was attached directly to his shoulders. He may not have coached his players to be cheap, but he never tried to stop them when things got out of hand.

Many years back, Jack and Ivan played against each other in the old USHL. Because of this, rumors were spread of a rivalry between the two coaches. Jack would shrug off any mention of animosity in the locker room, but when reporters asked questions he played it up. "It sells tickets," Jack told the guys.

Des Moines couldn't play a skating game with the Saints and expect to win, so they always did bizarre things to throw the guys off their game. The two worst delinquents were players we'll call Smiles and Dopey. Most of the Saints expected to see those two names in the newspaper headlines, in the court convictions section, at some point during the season. Those guys were bat-shit crazy.

Earlier in the season, the Saints heard a rumor that one of them threw a stick like a javelin into the bench at the St Paul Vulcan coach, splitting his head open. They played it off as another wild rumor until the St. Paul team came to Dubuque, and the coach looked like Frankenstein.

When the Saints played in Des Moines, Jack would advise them, "Be on your toes behind the play." The Buccaneers were good at waiting until the referee was looking away.

Early in the third period, Gibby had the puck in the corner and made a pass up the boards. He watched the play move up the ice. He didn't notice Dopey coming around the net throwing an elbow into his nose. In fact, he had no idea what hit him. The cheap shot dropped him to his knees. He got up but his eyes were watering so bad that he couldn't see where the bench was. He made out a fuzzy dark spot through half closed eyes and headed towards it hoping it was the right bench. Mel stopped Gibby as he put one leg into the Buccaneers bench, probably saving him from another beating.

The normal response to a cheap shot like that would have been a fight, and Mel was willing; but after regaining his vision Gibby told Mel, "It's my fault, I should have listened to Jack in the locker room. I'll get that son of a bitch later."

Other than a few behind the play cheap shots like that, the weekend series with the Buccaneers was surprisingly clean. No fights in either game. In this weekend series the Buccaneers tried to play a skill game of hockey, but it didn't work. The Saints embarrassed them in Dubuque 11-1, and then beat them soundly in Des Moines 6-3.

If there was a bitter rivalry between Jack and Crazy Ivan, it took the weekend off. The Saints dominated.

January 28th, 1981:

Austin 7, Saints 4 (away)

"Saints winning streak broken" -*Telegraph Herald*

After the loss to the Mavericks, Deano and Collins talked it over and agreed they should talk to Jack about it together. They walked into Jack's office after practice hoping to catch him in a good mood.

"We need you to get Scanny back here. He's a funny guy. We need that in the locker room," Deano said stating it as a matter of fact, not a request.

"You think that's why we lost to Austin?" Jack asked sarcastically.

Not amused, Deano replied, "Maybe. It's not as much fun without him around."

"Listen Jack, I don't think he knew how much he was a part of the team," Collins chimed in. "And our apartment is boring without him," he added.

Jack didn't want Scanny back if he wasn't going to get much playing time but maybe Scanny didn't realize how much he contributed in other ways than scoring goals, Scanny had yet to score a single goal. Then another thought entered Jack's mind, "Maybe I don't realize how much he contributed either."

"Ok, I'll give Anzalone a call. If he agrees to let him go, it will be up to Scanny to decide," Jack said.

Frank Anzalone, the Waterloo Black Hawks coach, agreed to give Scanny the facts and let him make the choice. "You can stay here and probably get more playing time, or you can go back to Dubuque. Jack said you would be in the same role as you were before you left. He also said there would be no guarantee of playing time."

Scanny was a hard-nose competitor, which is why Jack kept him around in the first place. His initial thought was to stay in Waterloo and get as much ice time as possible, but he liked the guys in Dubuque.

"Some of these guys in Waterloo are off-the-wall weird," he thought to himself. It was puzzling because that would indicate that he thought Worps and the rest of the Dubuque guys were normal. He let that sink in for several minutes then realized that the guys in Dubuque were strange too. They were strange in bizarre yet mostly honorable ways. Worps' insults were harmless and funny; Nordsy was naive but gutsy; Deano was tough but lovable; Collins was talented and quiet; Bulldog was awesome yet humble and Jack was a fair coach.

His decision was made. He would go back to Dubuque and make the best of it by being himself. The rest of it was out of his hands. He would give everything he could on every shift he was given.

A week later he was back in the Saints locker room, wearing the number "8" jersey and getting "noogie's" from Worps. "We love you, you knucklehead. Don't ever leave us again!" Worps said. (Author's note: If you older folks don't know what "noogie's" are, ask one of your grandkids to look it up on their smart phone.)

Scanny was confident he made the right the decision. Collins and Deano never told Scanny about their request to Jack.

January 30th, 1981:

Saints 10, Sioux City 1 (home)

"Saints fire 98 shots, bury Sioux City" - *Telegraph Herald*

When the whistle blew a Sioux City forward we'll call Jaws was pinned against the boards behind the Saints net by Gibby. As Gibby skated away Jaws shoved him in the back. Gibby turned around and loosened the glove on his left hand. He took a step closer to the Musketeer, and then let the glove slide off the instant his left hand started in motion towards Jaws' face.

For the most part hockey fights are harmless affairs. They usually result in two guys grabbing onto each other while throwing a few short punches that don't connect with anything but look like they might hurt if they did. Even a fight with Mel could result in a guy getting knocked down, a bloody lip or nose, but little else. Most of the time the only thing seriously injured in a hockey fight is the losing player's ego.

There is far more violence in a Curt Voegeli hip check or a Mel Bailey center ice collision than in an average USHL fight. Hip checks and collisions could result in season ending injuries. Fights usually ended with both combatants going to the ice where they would be given a nice little hug by the linesmen.

Few players went toe-to-toe in a fight. Toe-to-toe is a term where the players simultaneously grab the other with one hand while throwing as many punches as they can with the other until one of them connects or they get too tired from throwing punches. They then grab each other with both arms going to the ice where the linesmen separate them peacefully.

Gibby's brother, Mike, taught him how to win a hockey fight. Mike Gibbons was a slugger similar to Mel. Both Mike and Mel have been known to knock guys out with one solid punch. Those types of fighters were considered "killers" that could hurt an opponent. Much like Bulldog's scoring ability, it is very hard to teach someone to be a killer.

After he received the swollen knot on his forehead from Murphy in his first USHL fight, Gibby knew that he wasn't a killer and never would be. Jack knew that Gibby's brother Mike was a killer, so perhaps he thought it was a family trait...it wasn't.

The Gibbons family did have a fighting history though. Gibby's grandfather, Michael, was the boxing middleweight champion of the world with a 65-3-4 record in professional bouts. In 1909 the current middleweight champion was shot and killed in a bar fight, so Michael Gibbons claimed the title shortly afterward.

Boxing at that time was comprised of sluggers with matches lasting as long as someone was still standing. Michael was one of the first boxers to perfect the art of dodging a punch. The press nicknamed him the St. Paul Phantom for his defensive skills.

Barzee told Gibby early on that he was a true defenseman. Blocking shots and breaking up 2 on 1's is what he was good at, so he took pride in that. He also made defense a strategy in fighting. His fighting strategy was as follows:

1.) *Get in the first punch.*

2.) *Grab the guy's right arm so you don't get a knot on your forehead.*

3.) *Throw as many quick right-hand punches as you can.*

4.) *Wrestle the guy to the ground.*

5.) When the linesmen break up the fight, get up and claim victory.

It was a sound strategy that worked. If he thought he was in a fight with a killer, he would skip steps #1 and #3, choosing instead to grab both of his opponent's arms in a strictly defensive maneuver. It was also prudent to skip #5 in that situation, specifically the part about claiming victory.

It was before the Sioux City game that he planned on fighting with his left hand. Gibby wanted to try a different strategy. The fight against Jaws went as planned since he threw the first punch when he quickly slipped off his glove. He surprised Jaws with several more quick left hand punches, a few which connected solidly. At that point he should have gone to step #4, but he decided to keep throwing punches until Jaws went down. It was a mistake. The punches had no effect on Jaws, and Gibby had spent all his energy.

The combatants finally went to the ground with Jaws ending up on top. Gibby waited patiently for Stoltzy and Waddy to pull the crazed lunatic off when he felt a stabbing pain in his back. Jaws was firmly biting Gibby's shoulder blade.

"Aaaahhh! Get him off me," Gibby screamed. The pain was excruciating. It felt like the guy had ripped flesh off with his teeth.

In the locker room after the game Gibby had his back to the mirror trying to get a look at the wound but couldn't get a good view. "How bad is it?" he asked Bucky.

Bucky said, "It looks like you got Jaws' full dental impression, including molars." Gibby decided to call in Doc Field for a closer look.

After a quick observation Doc Field said, "It's a good one, but I wouldn't worry about it too much. Only a few teeth broke through the skin."

"Shouldn't I get a tetanus shot or something?" Gibby said fearing that the guy's salvia was poisonous.

Sensing Gibby's fear Doc Field decided to play along. "I suppose we could do a series of rabies shots. Come down to the office tomorrow. We'll get you started on the first ten."

Gibby couldn't tell if he was playing with his mind. "You aren't serious...are you Doc?" The locker room broke out in laughter at Gibby's expense. He never tried fighting left-handed again.

February 4th, 1981:

Saints 7, Green Bay 1 (home)

"Jasken narrowly misses shutout" -Telegraph Herald

NHL Hall of Fame goalie Ken Dryden once posed the question: "How would you like a job where, if you made a mistake, a big red light comes on and thousands of people boo?" Goalies are like football kickers, you usually see them sitting by themselves away from the rest of the team in their own little world. But just like football kickers, goalies can make or break a game. When they are playing good, they are complimented and praised. When they are playing bad, they are left alone in their own solitary misery.

Most goalies have unique personalities, which is a polite way of saying they are weird. Jask and Granger were two of those goalies with unique personalities.

Granger was the quintessential "field goal kicker." He and Walshy shared a room at the 11th Street apartments. Early in the season Granger decided he wanted a pet. He asked Walshy if he objected to having a cat in the apartment. Walshy did not object but wanted nothing to do with feeding or cleaning the animal. Later in the week Granger came home with a gray tabby and a collection of supplies. Much to Walshy's surprise the cat had one huge benefit. Girls liked to come over and see the cat. While they were there the girls would do dishes and clean up the apartment for them. Walshy had a steady girlfriend, but her friends would occasionally tag along to see the cat. Getting a cat was odd, but perhaps Granger knew what he was doing. Cats didn't need much attention and could be left unattended for long periods of time. The fact that girls were attracted was an added bonus.

Not to be outdone, the guys on Bluff Street decided they should get a dog. "Go to the animal shelter and get the ugliest short haired dog you can find," Worps instructed Reegs. They decided that getting a mascot dog would attract girls. "The uglier the dog, the more beautiful the girls it would attract," they rationalized.

Reegs didn't have to go to the animal shelter. A dog with no collar had been hanging around the block. They assumed it was a stray. Reegs brought it into the house after Worps agreed that it met the "short hair and ugly" requirement. Overnight it defecated on the third floor. On his way to the bathroom, Mel stepped in it. Frustrated and pissed, he wanted the dog gone. When Worps got back from practice, he found that the dog had chewed apart his treasured cowboy boots. Finally Worps and Mel agreed on something...the dog had to go. Reegs released the dog back out onto the street without ever giving it a name.

Jask was a fun loving goalie with an outgoing personality, but he did some strange things. It was common during a game to hear him whistling regularly and loudly from behind his goalie mask. He didn't whistle to any specific tune, it was just loud whistling.

This was Jask's way of warning the defensemen that they had an opposing player on their tail. It was a complicated warning system that he tried to explain to the defensemen; one long whistle for one guy pursuing you, two whistles meant two guys, and three quick whistles meant they were really close.

In the locker room, after Jask educated his defensemen on the system, Gibby turned to Bucky and Vogy. "You guys understand all that?" he asked in a soft voice so as not to offend Jask. Jask clearly went through a lot of strategizing to come up with his system.

"Yah, but it's all just white noise on the ice when I have my back turned," said Bucky.

"He whistles so damn much it's like they have too many men on the ice," said Vogy.

Overhearing the conversation Worps had to chime in, "I don't think Mel can count to three anyway." After a while the defense paid no attention to the whistles. In most of the situations, the defensemen were already aware of their predicament before the whistles started.

Before the Green Bay game, Gibby was going to let Jask know that his whistling was confusing; but Bucky stopped him. "Let him keep whistling. It makes him feel like he's helping. I think he concentrates better," advised Bucky. It was good advice; Jask almost shut out Green Bay that night. They never told Jask he was wasting his time and effort so the whistling continued.

Like all the players, Jask had a tough time sleeping on bus trips, but once comfortably home on his cot he could sleep through just about any noise the guys could make. Jask regularly slept while the other guys mulled about because the cot was located in the living room. About the only thing that could wake Jask was Granger's cat when it was feeling playful. The cat tormented Jask in the early morning hours with its claws.

"Look at him, he's out cold," said Bucky early one morning as Jask slept soundly on his cot. Vogy looked at Jask then got a terribly wonderful idea. He went back into his room digging through his duffel bag. He came out with two large rolls of hockey tape.

Together, Bucky and Vogy quietly wrapped the tape around Jask and the cot until both rolls were used up. Jask's arms, legs and body were pinned to the cot. Hockey tape doesn't stretch. Jask was still sound asleep.

Jask woke up, just as Bucky and Vogy were getting ready to leave for practice. "What the f--k!" Jask realized he was going nowhere without some help. "Aaaargh! Come on you guys, let me out," Jask pleaded. Bucky and Vogy left for practice, closing the door behind them without saying a word or acknowledging Jask's predicament. Jask made it to practice late with nasty ligature marks on his arms.

February 6ᵗʰ & 7ᵗʰ, 1981:

Saints 12, Sioux City 4 (away)

Saints 7, Sioux City 4 (away)

"Grillo's nine goals spark Saints sweep" -Telegraph Herald

The starting lineup almost always included the Bulldog line, but tonight was an exception. On Friday night the Grillo-Worps-DiNap line accounted for seven of twelve goals against Sioux City. The Bulldog line scored only two. Grillo himself scored five, three of those in the first period.

In the second game of the series, the Grillo line was introduced as the starters. Jack saw the damage they inflicted on Sioux City and he hoped it would happen again in the second game, but he was worried Grillo would be over confident.

Before the opening face-off he called Grillo over to the bench and grabbed him by the jersey, pulling him close. "Listen you piece of crap. I think you got lucky yesterday. You're going to go out there and skate laps thinking you're cool. I don't think you'll score another goal for a week!" He let go of his jersey and pointed towards center ice where the referee was waiting patiently.

Grillo was dumbfounded. He skated into position to take the opening face-off thinking, "What a jerk. That asshole doesn't appreciate anything I do for this team. I'll show that son of a bitch." His angst turned into anger.

The puck dropped and it took all of six seconds for Grillo to fire one past the Sioux City goalie. On his next shift he scored another goal. He completed the hat trick in the first period, just like he did the night before. He added one more in the final period for good measure. Jack Barzee, the Silver Fox, smiled after each goal. Grillo had no idea he had just been played like a proverbial fiddle.

Of all the bizarre player personalities and the quirkiness on the team, Jack Barzee, the coach, is the hardest to define. They called him the Silver Fox not because he was a great strategist or hockey genius but because he was a great psychologist. The "Silver" part was for his gray hair, "Coaching guys like this will do that to a guy," he said.

It was not uncommon for one or more of the players to be mad at Jack. In fact, there were few players that did not ask to be traded, or at least threaten to, at some point in the season. Most thought they were getting screwed by Jack; but to his credit, he didn't care. He knew they were idle threats. Good coaches don't set out to be liked by their players because it is of no consequence. Jack pushed each of his players to the edge so they could play beyond their abilities. If it meant that they hated him at times in the process then that was just part of the job.

Even if some players didn't like how they were being treated, many of those same players were overheard saying, "I would bang my head against the boards if Jack asked me to." It was a strange dichotomy that Jack seemed to intentionally create in their minds.

Several players from other teams said the success of the Saints was not necessarily the talent of the players but that of the coach. They thought that Jack had a great system that made the team win. The real truth is that Jack would take a competitive young athlete and allow them to succeed without a system. There was no system, unless you call Jack's psychology skills a system. Jack had a God given ability to get the best out of each player without taking a single psychology class or any post-secondary education. His knowledge came from decades of experiencing other player's success and failure on the ice and in the locker room.

In the USHL, Jack started by getting the right type of player in the first place. Jack kept players that had the drive to win. They needed to have the philosophy that they will never be out worked and possess an unbreakable drive to compete, no matter the circumstances. They also needed to be a team player, willing to sacrifice for the team and their teammates. Jack called it "True Grit."

Although Jack regularly got the type of player he wanted, if a player was lacking in a specific area he would try to get the player to improve. If they couldn't produce for the team, they would be traded or released. Producing was not about scoring goals or stopping goals, it was about drive. Mike Fallon scored 5 goals in the regular season in 1980-81. He came back and played for Jack after being diagnosed with Hodgkin's disease, a disease that would recur twice; and he defeated it each time. He continued to play at the Division I level and then professionally in Europe. That is the definition of True Grit, not scoring goals.

Jack knew that Scanny would go out onto the ice confident that he could do the job and help his team win. That is what Jack expected from every player on every shift. Somehow he got that from the players, without ever actually asking for it. Jack did not give great motivational speeches; he made sure his players were already sufficiently motivated before they put their skates on. Jack kept the game simple and preached the basics. He didn't have a championship system; he created a bunch of champions.

Finally, Jack wanted the game to be fun. "Winning is the only way to have fun in hockey. Playing a winning game is both satisfying and fun," Jack said. The real truth is that Jack allowed the kids to be kids. He let them make the same mistakes he made as a young player. This includes off the ice as well as in games. If a player engaged in off-ice activities that affected the team, that player would be gone. Although these players did plenty of stupid things, discipline was rarely needed.

Jack never had to be hard on the players because most of them were already too hard on themselves. Grillo was one exception, he worried Grillo would sit back and admire his accomplishments in the first Sioux City game. Like a professional psychologist, trained in the science of the adolescent brain, the Silver Fox put Grillo in the right mindset to succeed with a simple tug on his jersey and a few "motivational" words.

February 14th & 15th, 1981:

Saints 8, St. Paul 3 (home)

Saints 11, Sioux City 2 (home)

"Saints whip St. Paul to give Barzee birthday present" -*Telegraph Herald*

They beat the St. Paul Vulcans 9-4 on Valentine's Day setting up February 15th as their first opportunity to clinch the Anderson Cup, the USHL regular season championship; and the right to have their individual names engraved on the trophy for eternity. Some of the players were over confident; others were nervous. They knew they would win it eventually, but they didn't want to lay an egg on home ice in front of 2600 loyal fans. By now they were expected to win every night. That put a lot of pressure on the players to perform. For some it was overwhelming, for others, not so much.

Deano and Collins were too laid back to feel pressure; put them in the "over confident" column. Nordsy, Gibby, Bulldog, Walshy, Fallon and Jasky felt the pressure; put them in the "nervous" column. Bucky, Vogy, Badger and Gringo were over confident. Granger, DiNap and Scanny: nervous. Reegs and Guy were on the fence. Mel? Mel just wanted to kill opponents so put him in with Reegs and Guy. Not sure about Worps. He may have felt the pressure but never showed it. His method of handling pressure was to belittle the opposing teams and players. "The Kamikaze is a weasel," or "The Mad-Dicks," his term for the Austin Mavericks, "are a bunch of pathetic losers." Other times he would belittle himself and his teammates in the same sentence, "Obviously you passed the puck to the wrong guy if you were expecting a goal...idiot." He belittled everyone all the time so you couldn't tell if the pressure was getting to him.

The guys who were over confident had every reason to be. They were playing the Sioux City Musketeers to clinch the Cup. "Sewage City Mouseketeers" to Worps. Sewage City wasn't very good. But the nervous guys had reason to be nervous too. The Mouseketeers had beaten the Saints before, giving them one of their first losses of the season; and recently, they beat the second place Mad-Dicks.

If you know anything about hockey players, you would know that most of them are superstitious to the extreme. They have the same pre-game rituals for every game. They put their equipment on the same way every time. If they didn't, that could cost them the game. Sometimes they went to extremes to prevent bad omens from affecting the games. Earlier in the season Gibby was driving a date home after a night out. A black cat crossed the road two blocks from her house. He stopped the car and made her walk from there. They never dated again. Today was different. He played his pre-game song on his 8-track tape player, put his Irish green towel around his neck and headed to the arena feeling good about his rituals. In the locker room, Scanny tied his left skate first. Uh oh...that was a mistake. He took off both skates and started over. Worps always put his skates on first, then tugged everything else on over the blades; no one really knows why.

The players were expecting Coach Barzee to give some sort of inspiring pre-game speech warning them not to be over confident or scolding them to keep focused on the task at hand. In the locker room the players fidgeted noisily as they finished getting ready.

When Coach Barzee walked in, the locker room became eerily silent. The players looked up at Barzee waiting for their inspiration. Barzee paced a few steps, took a deep breath and started the speech. "Listen up guys," he said, then he paused for dramatic effect. "We've got the Cup here and after the game we'll take pictures, but I don't want anybody picking it up or trying to carry it. And no one's going to drink from it!"

Put Barzee in the over confident column.

The speech put Gibby over the top. "But Coach, what about the game?" he said.

"Oh, we'll win the game. I just don't want it to be a circus afterwards." That was the extent of Barzee's motivational speech. It was probably the best speech of his career. They won the game 11-2.

On the ice after the game there was emotional celebration and revelry, but it was organized and disciplined. No one grabbed the cup or carried it over their heads. Bucky wanted to go up in the stands with his skates on, but Vogy stopped him.

They took a team picture with the cup, making sure the raucous fans were in the background. Then they left the ice pointing up into the crowd thanking them for their support. In the locker room the real celebration began. Corks were popped and beer cans were opened. Nordsy even drank some, well maybe...he was sprayed with it and some got into his mouth. Hugs and slaps on the back, hooting and hollering!

Jasky was near the door and heard a noise from outside. "Hey guys...you hear that?" he said as he opened the door. "Listen...they want us back out there! Let's go!" They came back out, skates still on, some half undressed with champagne bottles in hand. They took a few more victory laps with their fans. The hockey people in Dubuque had earned the right to celebrate just as much as the players. Unfortunately, they didn't have enough champagne for all of them. They took a couple bonus laps while Barzee hurried the trophy away to safety.

After the locker room celebration ended, the guys showered and went out to continue the celebration. Gibby and Worps went home to Bluff Street to drop off their bags, and then went to a couple downtown bars, but they couldn't find any of the other guys. They went to the Walnut Tap, but no one was there.

Finally, they went back to the house, had a few more beers and went to bed. There was nothing else to do on a Sunday night in Dubuque.

It's actually quite common for sports teams after winning a championship at home to be pulled in all different directions by a variety of forces. Family, friends, fans and all kinds of activities pull teammates away from each other after the immediate euphoria. Worps and Gibby wanted the locker room celebration to last all night, but it ended when they left the Five Flags Center.

February 19th, 20th & 21st, 1981:

Saints 5, Austin 5 (away)

St. Paul 4, Saints 3 (away)

Green Bay 7, Saints 6 (away)

"Fighting Saints lose two" -Telegraph Herald

They won the Anderson Cup on Sunday. Monday was a workday with no practice scheduled. They skipped work and slept late. At 11:30 AM Worps was next door at the ladies house watching his soap operas. Grillo and Bulldog were sitting in the living room drinking a beer. "Its past noon out East" said Dinap as he joined in. "Kishhhh," it made that sound when he tugged on the pull-top can.

Gibby thought Badger went into work then saw him coming down the stairs. "It's awesome outside guys! It's like 70 degrees out! My window opens far enough for us to get out on the roof. Feels like 80 in the sun!" Badger exclaimed with excitement. Grillo grabbed the remaining beer and followed Badger back to his room. They slipped through the window onto the sun drenched asphalt roof with their shirts off getting a suntan. It was February 16th, 1981, and it was 68 degrees in Dubuque.

Several of the guys from the 11th Street apartments came over. They spent the entire day out on that roof. They stacked Old Style beer cans in pyramids as they emptied them. When they ran out they went to the beer store and got more. It was an unusual heat wave for February, and the guys made the best of it.

Just before dark a motorcycle gang complete with tattoos and biker chicks drove up the alley and parked in back. "I don't think these guys are hockey fans, this could be trouble," said Bulldog.

"Hey dudes, you guys got any beer?" said Grillo looking over the few beers left on the roof. They didn't answer. Soon Badger went down to inquire what they were doing in their alley. After a while several of the other guys went down to join Badger in the alley. They thought that if the biker's didn't beat the crap out of Badger, it was probably safe for the rest of them.

It turned out that the biker gang didn't drink. They were also nice people. "Damn, even the biker gangs are nice in Dubuque!" said Gibby. They hung out with them for hours. The hockey players were intrigued with the biker lifestyle, and the bikers were intrigued with the hockey lifestyle.

The heat wave went on for another couple days and another couple days of tanning on the Badgers roof. Badger thought that the heat wave was awesome, and it was sweet that it coincided with the Saints winning the Cup; but he also thought it was sad for the kids in the city of Dubuque. The outdoor rinks were reduced to puddles. Hockey had grown in this town because of the Saints. Now the kid's outdoor season was cut short by this unusual heat wave.

They had three days of celebration then it was back to business. They went to Austin on Thursday for the start of a tough three game road trip. In the second period Granger got into a pushing match behind the net with a blond curly haired Austin player. Granger hit him with his stick, and Gibby jumped in immediately knocking "Curly" to the ground. Gibby got in a few punches with his gloves still on. He was ejected from the game for third man entering an altercation. "That wasn't even a fight!" Gibby argued to no avail, the referee's decision stood.

It just so happened that "Curly" was now dating Badgers old high school sweetheart. Worps, Reegs and Gibby knew Badger's old flame from the previous year.

Gibby slowly walked through the empty lobby after leaving the ice, feeling like he had been ripped off. "I barely touched the guy," he thought. As he got close to the locker room, Badger's old flame came running down the lobby screaming at him, "Gibby, you better not have done that because of me!" She was red faced with anger and out of breath from the jog.

"It wasn't about you. He hit my goalie! Jeez, get over yourself," Gibby said and slipped through the locker room door letting it slam behind him. He sat down in the empty locker room and got undressed. He thought about what Badger's old flame just said, and how red-faced mad she was. He laughed out loud, no longer feeling bad about getting thrown out of the game.

After overtime the Austin game remained tied. The Saints then went to St. Paul where they lost a close one. The next game in Green Bay was the same result. This was the only time the Saints lost two in a row. It seemed the Saints might have lost their edge. There was no reason to panic, they were one-goal games, but they normally won those types of games.

Jack and Clarence allowed beer on the bus ride home. It was a bad idea. When they unloaded at the Five Flags Center, it was past three in the morning and some of the guys were still tipsy.

"Practice tomorrow at 8 AM sharp!" Jack said before they departed for their homes. They normally skipped the regular 8 a.m. practice after long bus rides.

"What the f--k is that all about?" asked Grillo back at the Bluff Street house. "It's not like we got blown out. Screw it," he said and went to the fridge to have another beer. Worps and Gibby joined him.

160

As 8 a.m. approached Grillo and Worps decided they would protest the practice by wearing their bathrobes out on the ice. Those who owned robes joined in. The guys were out on the ice in full-length bathrobes when Jack entered the ice surface. He was not impressed but said nothing. He had them do some drills but soon saw that there was no effort, so he decided to make them skate until they puked. Grillo turned into the corner and misjudged the distance to the boards. He hit the boards with a loud crash and fell to the ice giggling, obviously still intoxicated.

Jack had enough. He dragged Grillo by his robe over to the gate and threw him towards the locker room. "You're done; get outta here!"

Jack ran a few more drills then skated the team for a little while, but it was clear it was futile. He skated off the rink without saying a word. The rest of the team stood around not sure what to do. Reegs and Mel ran a few more drills, and then practice was done. You could hear a pin drop in the locker room as they got undressed. Normally, the guys had in-depth conversions in the shower; but today nobody said a word. The only noise was the water splashing against the cement floor. It was a wakeup call for the whole team. There was a lot more hockey to be played, and none of them liked losing.

February 25th, 1981:

Saints 6, Des Moines 0 (Home)

"Jasken records Saints first shutout" -*Telegraph Herald*

Home Sweet Home! There is nothing like a few days rest then playing a game on home ice. They dominated the Des Moines Buccaneers recording their first shutout of the season. They now had the league's top two scorers and the top two goalies, plus the highest scoring defenseman in Chris Guy.

Guy was silently racking up points by joining the rush up ice, making great passes and making his opportunities count. He was always the quiet one in the locker room, mainly because he sat next to Bucky; there was no talking over Bucky. If Guy wanted to make a comment, he had to wait for Bucky to stop talking...that could be a long wait, so he rarely bothered.

In the second period Chris Guy got in his first USHL fight. Smiles crosschecked Guy in front of the Des Moines bench then dropped his gloves. Apparently, Smiles was tired of Guy making them look bad. Surprisingly, Guy obliged Smiles by fighting back. Smiles was a competent fighter. He had run-ins with Worps, Gibby, Nordmark, and even a couple fights with Mel. Guy didn't win the fight but he didn't lose either. The 165-pound Chris Guy threw a few punches then frustrated Smiles by hugging him until they were separated by the linesmen. He escaped without a scratch.

That is the type of action quiet leaders take when the team needs a spark to lift them out of a slump. It wasn't much of a fight, but he earned a greater respect from his teammates by showing he wasn't going to back down from a "goon."

Jack created a special promotion for this game called "Autograph Night." He advertised it in the newspaper several times after they won the Anderson Cup. It was bad timing, coming off the terrible road trip the week before. The players never thought it would amount to much more than a few young kids with their parents.

Surprisingly, a huge crowd greeted them as they came out of the locker room, still wearing their sweaty jerseys and hockey gear. The plan was to have the player's line up in the outer lobby, but the fans gathered outside the locker room. The whole lobby area was filled with autograph seekers, as well. It was a mad house with people shoving the "Special Autograph Edition" programs at the players for signatures; even the linesmen Stoltzy and Waddy signed a few.

"This autograph ain't gonna be no good unless I get elected to the Senate, and we all know that ain't never gonna happen!" Jask said as he signed.

The autograph session went on for more than an hour after the game. Jack finally cut it off to let the players go home. That night actually helped the players understand their situation. They did not let any of it go to their heads. It was clear that the fans were infatuated with hockey in Dubuque. It was a fun time for all. They appreciated the accolades but were focusing on the larger goal.

The Des Moines game was the start of an 11 game winning streak that would carry them through the rest of the season and into the playoffs.

Autograph night at the Five Flags Center: In front of the
locker room (top), the packed lobby (bottom).

February 28th & March 1st, 1981:

Saints 7, Waterloo 3 (home)

Saints 7, Waterloo 5 (away)

"Saints beat Waterloo, Jasken, Guy injured" -*Telegraph Herald*

Chris Guy carried the puck around the defenseman and charged at the goalie. He made a great move to get behind the goalie, but the other defenseman came across and took him off his feet. He crashed into the goal post back first.

"Don't move him!" shouted the Waterloo medical professional as he rushed out onto the ice. This was the second game in the Home-and-Home series with the Black Hawks. The Saints beat Waterloo by four goals the night before.

The EMT held Guy by his helmet while he talked him through the checklist to make sure there was no permanent damage. Guy was in pain, but all his appendages were functional. After passing this paralysis test, Bucky gingerly escorted his defensive partner back to the bench where the EMT would examine him further.

Back in those days if a player could get up, he would be moved to the bench so as not to slow down the game. The concept of being "precautionary" was not used very often in the early 80's, at least not with the Saints. Concussions were not a big deal either. After a crushing blow, if a player had enough balance to stand up on his own and knew where he was, he would be back out on the ice for the next shift. It wasn't better or worse back then; it was just a different time with fewer things to worry about. Season ending injuries happened regularly, but not to the Saints. They were extremely lucky in that respect.

Later in the game Jask was screened on a slapshot from the point. He never saw the puck coming at him. He only felt the pain in his, um, "groin" area. The puck hit at the bottom of his cup, which smashed against his scrotum. He fell to the ice screaming in pain.

Once again the EMT came out onto the ice to assess the situation. Jask continued to scream in pain. With a latex glove on, the EMT reached down into Jask's breezers to examine the damage. There was something missing.

"Move back guys, I think we may have lost a testicle!" the EMT proclaimed searching around inside the hockey pants and on the ice for the missing, um..."ball."

Through his grinding teeth, holding back the pain, Jask grunted, "I only have one."

"What?" replied the EMT.

"I only have one ...it never dropped," Jask muttered. The EMT looked puzzled, he still didn't get it.

"When I was born...I only have one testicle!" Jask said louder and clearer.

The EMT's facial expression changed. He was working desperately not to laugh at his own mistake when Bucky, standing nearby, said, "We didn't think he had any, at least you found one!"

They all got a laugh; even Jask chuckled as the pain finally began to subside. He would miss the rest of the game and the "area" would be tender for another week or two, but everything was where it was before he got hit with the puck.

During the third period an unruly fan was riding Scanny. He was heckling him relentlessly. "You suck Scanlan! We never wanted you anyway!" Scanny ignored the imbecile.

The heckler was waiting for Scanny to come off the ice at the end of the game, but Scanny kept his head down and avoided eye contact. "Scanlan, I stole your fucking stereo and it's a piece of shit!" That got Scanny's attention. His head immediately popped up, seeking out the verbal villain.

When Scanny came to play in Waterloo for two weeks, someone broke into his car and stole his stereo. Scanny rarely got angry, but now he was furious. Still in his skates he ran across the concrete into the stands chasing after the guy, but the heckler bolted up the stairs. Scanny never caught up to him.

"If it makes you feel any better, I think Reegs slept with that guy's wife last year," said Worps, trying to lighten the situation. Scanny let out a small grin trying to put it behind him. He had to get undressed quickly because he was supposed to meet up with his Waterloo boarding family in the lobby after the game. Scanny only stayed with them a couple weeks, but he wanted to thank them for their hospitality before the team headed back to Dubuque.

Scanny was the first one to the bus. He threw his bag into the under-storage compartment on the bus, and then went back into the arena to talk with the family. Scanny talked with them for a few moments, thanked them one more time, and then went back outside. When he arrived at the bus, all the other players were still in the arena. He noticed his hockey bag was missing from the storage compartment.

"You've got to be kidding me!" He checked with the bus driver but he didn't know anything about it. He checked to make sure one of the guys wasn't playing a bad practical joke on him. They weren't. Someone in Waterloo has now stolen his car stereo and his hockey bag.

"If it makes you feel any better, the guy is gonna have to get those skates sharpened before he uses them," said Worps. This time he wasn't trying to console Scanny, he was rubbing salt into the wound.

Scanny didn't miss a practice. The next day, Jack got him a full set of new equipment, including skates. By the next game he had a new #8 jersey ready for him in the locker room.

March 4th, 1981:

Saints 6, Austin 3 (home)

"Carlson breaks record as Saints triumph" -*Telegraph Herald*

Late in the third period, Bulldog took a pass from Collins on the left side of the slot. He should have taken a shot; but he held onto the puck, drawing the sprawling Austin goalie and three defenders scrambling towards him. Still holding onto the puck, he circled around the goal frame, using it as a blocker. He rounded the net and put in a backhand from a sharp angle. The Saints bench cleared to congratulate Mike Bulldog Carlson on his record setting achievement.

That play broke the USHL single season scoring record on March 4th, 1981. The old record was 121 points. Bulldog came into the game needing one point to tie and two to break it. He tied it in the first period. He scored the record breaker with six minutes remaining in the game. He would add four more goals and another assist in the last game of the season to set the new single season record at 127 points.

Almost forty years later, Bulldog is listed number three for all-time single season point scorer in the USHL and still number one for the Dubuque Fighting Saints. Brian Collins tally of 108 points ranks eighth in the USHL and third in Dubuque.

As an individual achievement, the record didn't mean much to the team. There was no big celebration or trophy to hand out. Basically, the mark got him some pats on the back and extra "noogie's" from Worps.

Bulldog didn't dwell on it all. The unassuming kid from Two Harbors, Minnesota, was a down-to-earth guy. He would never garner accolades for any of his goals. "The puck just went in." "I got lucky on that one." "The goalie gave me half the net." These were some of the things he would say when he was bragging. When he was being humble, he would change the subject.

The guys would look at him in the locker room and wonder how he could do it. He didn't have the modern athletic build or blazing speed; he simply had "hockey sense." He knew where the puck was going to go before it got there. He also knew how to avoid getting hit. If he did get hit, he would turn his skates to be able to move with the check.

"Did you wear those elbow pads in Peewee's?" Bucky asked Bulldog. Bulldog's elbow pads were too small for even a Peewee player, but that was all he could afford. Bulldog was besieged by elbow injuries all season long. Bulldog had regular bumps and bruises, but no injuries that required him to sit-out a game.

At the Bluff Street apartment, Bulldog had his own room. The mattress sat on the floor and he used his suitcase as his dresser drawer. There was no nightstand, the alarm clock sat on the hardwood floor.

Bulldog worked during the day, like most of the guys, to pay the rent and for food. To cut corners he used the house dish soap to wash his hair. Gibby convinced Bulldog to get a perm, a method to have your hair permanently curled; because he had straight hair and a bowl haircut when he came to Dubuque.

Later in the season one of the guys had to make a trip to the drug store to get something you can only buy at a drug store. He did not want to be seen or recognized buying what he needed, so he grabbed Bulldog's Fighting Saints jacket. The coat said "BULLDOG" in big letters on the left front of the coat. He put on some dark sunglasses and a "Saints" ball cap to make the purchase incognito. It wasn't Bulldog, but the lady cashier thought it was.

The fans in Dubuque loved Bulldog and his "aw-shucks" humble attitude. Around town, kids would see him and ask for his autograph. In between periods at a home game, Bulldog coached (in an honorary role) an adult league broomball team against Jack Barzee. When the PA announcer noted Bulldog's name as coach, the crowd went wild. The Bulldog-Barzee match ended in a 1-1 tie.

Bulldog never let any of the fame get into his head. He remained a humble, levelheaded kid, even though he had every opportunity to let his ego swell. He was a very likable guy throughout the season. Bulldog was also a team player. He and Collins carried the team as an example of how to handle the fame and pressure of a successful season. They never lost sight of who they really were.

March 7th, 1981:

Awards Banquet, Five Flags Ballroom

"Keep things in the proper perspective" -Herb Brooks

For scheduling reasons the season ending awards banquet was held a day before the last regular season game. Players, fans and distinguished guests gathered for the prime rib dinner in the Five Flags Ballroom.

It was a formal affair so most of the guys dressed up in a suit and tie. Some of the guys didn't have anything nice to dress up in, so they begged and borrowed what they needed. Some either refused to wear a tie or couldn't get their hands on one. Gibby and Walshy didn't have dress shirts, so they wore turtlenecks underneath a borrowed suit coat.

The event was sold out, mainly because Herb Brooks was the guest speaker. Herb Brooks coached Team USA to the Olympic gold medal "Miracle on Ice" the year prior, so he was still a celebrity in the hockey world. Herb's close friend, Paul Johnson, one of the leading scorers of the 1960 gold medal winning Olympic team, was the other speaker. Paul and Jack were good friends and line-mates for the Waterloo Blackhawks in the late 60's, which led to Jack and Herb becoming good friends. The Dubuque hockey community, as well as the players, considered it an honor and a privilege to have both of them speak at the team banquet with the "Miracle on Ice" still in the spotlight.

After the opening ceremonies Ambassadors of the city of Dubuque presented each player with a "Key to the City" plaque. If those Ambassadors knew some of the things these players did off the ice in the last six months, they would not have trusted them with the key to the city.

Next up was the presentation of awards: MVP, Scoring Leader, Best Defenseman, Rookie of the Year, and Sportsmanship award. Everyone knew that the scoring leader was Bulldog, but the others were a secret until they were announced.

The MVP also went to Bulldog, no surprise there. The Best Defenseman went to Chris Guy, Rookie of the Year to Brian Collins, and the Sportsmanship was awarded to Worps. The latter was a shocker, especially since the players voted on it. Apparently, his insults didn't offend everyone on the team.

Each winner stepped up to the podium to accept the award and was asked to give a short speech. Each one politely thanked their teammates, the coach and the fans; and then stepped away from the microphone quickly, except for Worps. Worps never missed an opportunity to make fun of someone.

Worps' speech went like this: "The sportsmanship award usually goes to some pathetic loser who sucks, but his teammates feel sorry for him. I want to thank my teammates for thinking of me." There was mix of oooh's and aaah's combined with laughing. True to form Worps entertained the crowd.

Herb Brooks stepped up to the microphone soon after Worps and said, "I'm glad they never gave me a sportsmanship award."

Herb followed with a classic speech. He thanked those for inviting him and spoke highly of his friend Jack. He talked briefly about the Olympic team and the experience. When he was talking directly to the players, he said, "I told the Olympic team that they need to keep things in the proper perspective. It was only one game. There will be many more games and challenges for the rest of your lives that you will have to live up to. The same is true for you players. The season is still young. You have many more games to play, and they are only just games. When you have success like this, you need to keep it all in the proper perspective. Don't get too high on yourself, because there will be many more challenges ahead. Not just in hockey but out in the working world, and for the rest of your lives. Appreciate the moment, but keep it in perspective."

The comparison could be drawn that Herb got the most out of his Olympic players; much like Jack has done with the Saints. Apparently, to be a good coach you also needed to be a good psychologist. Herb and Jack were two of the best.

Worps, Dinap, Guy (Left to right) dressed-up with the Anderson Cup.

March 8th, 1981:

Saints 11, Sioux City 3 (home)

"Saints go easy on Sioux City in tune-up for playoffs" -Telegraph Herald

The final accomplishment for the team would be to win the last game of the regular season, thereby setting one more record for the fewest losses of any USHL team in the history of the league. Once again they were playing Sioux City on home ice. Sioux City only brought over nine skaters and goalie, so it was almost a forgone conclusion that the Saints would win.

But there was another task that needed to be taken care of. Playing mostly defense, Scanny had not gotten a goal all season, and it was his birthday. It was down to the final half of the final period when Scanny stepped over the blue line and took a hard wrist shot that hit a Musketeer player and bounced into the net. The Saints bench erupted in celebration, as they had in the previous game when Bulldog broke the scoring record. Once again the bench cleared for a celebration. The game was delayed for a several minutes. This time, however, the referee was not impressed with the outburst of enthusiasm in an 8-1 game. He gave the Saints a delay-of-game penalty.

"Scanny, take your puck and go serve the penalty," Jack said. The guys gave Scanny the puck to commemorate the goal.

Scanny just scored the first goal of his USHL career on the last game of the season, in the last period, on his twentieth birthday, and coach Barzee makes him serve the penalty. Wow! Others volunteered to take his place in the box, but Scanny saw it as a badge of honor.

At the end of the game Scanny was named the First Star of the game and given a five-pound can of ham for his efforts. At about the halfway point in the season, the team instituted a player recognition program where the three stars of the game would get prizes. The first star always got a five-pound can of ham, packaged right here in Dubuque. Needless to say, Bulldog and Collins ate well in the latter half of the season; but the cans were awarded to lots of other players as well. It became a means of subsistence at the player's homes.

Scanny would not be eating this ham. He brought the can home and put it on his shelf as a trophy. After the season ended he brought it home to New Jersey. For a decade, every place he lived, the canned ham sat on his mantle as a proud reminder of his season in Dubuque...until he got married. His wife decided that a can of ham was not something that should go in a living room.

Scanny reluctantly put the ham in his closet with his other Saints memorabilia. Late one summer night, while Scanny and his wife were sleeping, they heard a loud noise, which startled them awake. Scanny reluctantly got out of bed to make sure nobody was trying to break into their home. "It's nothing. Probably just the house shifting," Scanny said. It was an extremely hot August day and they didn't have air conditioning. Thinking nothing of it they went back to sleep only to wake up in the morning to the smell of rotting ham coming from the closet. Apparently the noise that jolted them awake was the sound of a fifteen-year-old five-pound can of rotting ham exploding in their closet. All their clothes needed to be cleaned and the closet fumigated. Scanny's trophy became a curse that left an odor in the bedroom for months.

Chapter 5: Playoffs

March 11ᵗʰ, 1981:

Saints 9, Green Bay 3 (home)

"Five-goal third period lifts Saints" -*Telegraph Herald*

Jack was anticipating a full house but only 1272 fans showed up for the first home playoff game in Dubuque history. A factor could have been caused by the round-robin format, which means the Saints would play five games in eleven days, three of them at home. Perhaps the absent fans were waiting for the final series. If the Saints finished in the top two of the round-robin phase, they would advance to the final series of the Clark Cup. The first obstacle would be Green Bay, the only team to beat the Saints three times during the regular season.

Before the game the players were in the locker room going through their pre-game rituals. Most were nervous to be starting out with their toughest opponent, but some were taking it in stride. Collins was as cool as a cucumber, as he always is; and Worps was using his sarcasm to keep the guys loose. "Maybe I'll let that goon beat me up again," Worps said, referring to the fight he had the last time the Saints played in Green Bay. Worps dropped his gloves and went after one of the toughest Bobcat players on the team. It was a mistake.

The puck was dropped in the first home playoff game in Dubuque history, giving way to two periods of back and forth action. The score had the Saints up 4-3 going into the third period, when all hell broke loose for the Bobcats. Collins started the scoring off less than two minutes in. He was followed by three other Saints' goals in less than seven minutes.

With more than 12 minutes left in the game, the Bobcats had given up. They decided to rest future NHL goalie and current Minnesota Wild goalie coach, Bob Mason, in preparation for their next opponent. The Saints won 9 to 3.

March 14th, 1981:

Saints 11, Des Moines 5 (away)

"Regan's hat trick helps Saints post playoff victory" -*Telegraph Herald*

The next game was in Des Moines. Rivalries don't normally matter in playoff hockey, but they knew this would be a battle, and the game would take a physical toll on their bodies. The goal was to leave there as quickly as possible with two points for the win and zero injuries.

There were 46 penalties called which included three 5-minute majors, six misconducts, and a match penalty. The match penalty was given to a Buccaneer player in the second period for elbowing Reegs behind the play. It was very similar to the cheap shot Gibby received earlier in the season, but this time the linesman saw it and reported it to the referee.

The injury sent Reegs to the locker room for observation. In the first period Reegs scored a beautiful goal and was dominating play in the offensive zone. He returned to the game in the third period, scored two more goals to complete the hat trick, and then was the first player on the bus. "Let's get the f--k outta this hell hole and never come back!" said the embattled Reegs.

The Saints win virtually eliminated any hopes of Des Moines making the finals. It was a very satisfying feeling. Maybe rivalries do matter in the playoffs.

March 18th, 1981:

Saints 7, Austin 4 (home)

"Saints take big step toward playoff final" -*Telegraph Herald*

Once again it was a tight game going into the third period, but Bulldog and Collins scored two goals in six seconds in the seventh minute of the third period to seal the victory. After the game the discussion in the locker room turned to more important topics than playoff hockey. The popular rock band, Cheap Trick, was going to be playing at the Five Flags Center tomorrow; and the players needed to get tickets.

"Hey Jackie-boy, you got some pull around here. Why don't you swing us some tickets for the big win tonight?" asked Bucky, never shy to request handouts from Jack.

"That's a City thing. You guys are on your own," replied Jack.

Worps and Reegs previously arranged for free entrance to the concert. They volunteered to sell T-shirts for the backup band. The other guys needed to find a way to get tickets because they cost nine dollars. That was more than most could afford, and a Cheap Trick concert was not considered a necessity.

Back at the Bluff Street house, Gibby came up with devious plan. Tomorrow they had practice early in the morning, after which the city workers would cover the ice in preparation for the concert stage. The plan was to take a few things home in their team issued hockey bags. Then sometime in the afternoon they would go back to the arena while the stage was being set up, stay in the locker room until the band started playing, and then walk out into the concert like they were regular paying concertgoers.

"I'm in but what the heck are we going to do for 4 hours?" asked Bulldog.

"When we bring our bags back in with us, we can smuggle in some beer," Grillo proposed brilliantly.

On Thursday, March 19th, 1981, the devious plan was set in motion. They tried to enlist a few others, but no one else was interested in sitting in the locker room for that long. At 2pm, Gibby, Grillo and Bulldog, dressed in their Saints jackets, went through the front doors of the Five Flags arena and asked to go to the Saints locker room to drop off the hockey bags. Inside one of the bags, they smuggled in a twelve-pack of Old Style beer.

Once inside the locker room, they hid the beer then waited for an hour with the lights on and the door unlocked to see if the guy that let them in would check up on them. Feeling secure that the guy didn't care or got busy with other tasks; it was time to put the rest of the plan in motion. They locked the door and turned the lights off. They waited for a couple more hours occasionally opening a beer slowly so as not to make too much noise. Conversations were whispers. They only had a twelve pack, so they had to stretch that out over the long waiting period. They also had to hide the cans before leaving.

Every once in a while they would hear people walking by the door and talking, but no one noticed them in the dark locker room. Security was more concerned with the perimeter; they probably never expected an inside job. When the backup band started playing, the three Saints waited another half hour before removing their Saints jackets and entering the arena as regular music fans. They pulled off a cheap trick on Cheap Trick.

March 20th, 1981:

Saints 6, St Paul 3 (home)

"Late scoring gives Saints win over St. Paul" -Telegraph Herald

St. Paul scored with thirteen minutes left in the third period to tie the game, silencing the nineteen hundred fans in attendance. It took until the last 2 minutes and twenty seconds for Collins to get the game winner. But the most exciting goal did not come from Collins, or Bulldog, or even Scanny. In fact, this player had never scored a goal to that point in his career, not in the USHL and not in high school.

St. Paul dumped the puck into the Saints zone with less than two minutes remaining. They chased it down in the corner, but it squirted free in front of the net. No one was near the right side of the net, so Jask stepped out of his crease and cleared the puck out of the zone. In the meantime the St. Paul goalie went to the bench for the extra attacker.

Jask's clearing attempt made it past the St. Paul defenders and took an angle towards the empty net. One St. Paul defender dove at the puck but was too late. Mark Jasken scored his first goal as a goalie. It was the first recorded goal by a goalie in the USHL playoff history. The home crowd went crazy.

Deano added an extra open net goal to make the final score 6-3. This victory assured the Saints the top spot in the Clark Cup final series and a trip to the National Tournament in April. Having a goalie score a playoff goal was one more thing to check off on the list of records to be set in the season.

March 22nd, 1981:

Saints 8, Waterloo 7 (away)

"Saints complete playoff sweep" -*Telegraph Herald*

The Saints had to make the trip to Waterloo to play the final game of the round-robin series. The game meant nothing for the Saints, but Waterloo still had a chance to qualify for the final spot in the Clark Cup finals. They needed to win and then get some help from Des Moines by having them beat Austin.

For Barzee it would be bittersweet to eliminate his former organization; but this was not personal, it was business. The players that played in Waterloo the year before would be playing for the last time in their former arena, and they wanted to win. Many die-hard fans made the two-hour trip to watch the game.

It was a spirited game and the Black Hawks played with desperation. The Black Hawks led by a goal late in the third period. As was the case throughout the season when goals were needed, someone stepped up to the plate. This time it was defenseman, Mel Bailey.

In one of Jack's brilliant coaching moves, he put Mel at forward in the third period. No one knows why Jack did it. Mel scored only 3 goals all season.

With less than five minutes left in the game, Mel scored his fourth goal of the year. Three minutes later he silenced the home crowd by scoring the game-winner. The Saints won 8-7. Mel Bailey's two-goal scoring streak ended the Black Hawks season and sent the Saints into the Clark Cup finals undefeated.

Clark Cup Series

March 24th-April 3rd, 1981:

Game 1: Saints 6, Austin 3 (home)

Game 2: Austin 5, Saints 4 (away)

Game 3: Saints 5, Austin 3 (home)

Game 4: Saints 5, Austin 4 (Mankato, MN)

"Saints win Clark Cup on late goal by Worpell" -*Telegraph Herald*

It was down to the final two weeks in Dubuque for the players. Since they had qualified for the National Tournament, plans were being made for the trip to Green Bay, where the tournament was being hosted, but they tried to stay focused on winning the Clark Cup. They needed to beat the Austin Mavericks three times in a best of five series to earn the title.

Like most of the other contests, the Saints waited until the third period to pour it on in the first match with Austin. The third period started tied, but Bulldog got one early and Collins added two in the latter half. The game would end 6-3. It was the perfect start for the series.

The next game was in Austin; and if not for a late goal that was denied by the referee, the game would have gone into overtime. The loss ended the Saints winning streak at eleven. Not to be deterred, the Saints won the next game at home by a score of 5-3, once again waiting until later in the third period to put the Mavericks away.

The next and possibly the last game of the series could have been played in Dubuque because Austin's home arena was not available. Instead, Austin chose to host the game at a neutral site in Mankato, Minnesota.

On March 24th, when the puck dropped in Mankato, the stands were filled with two busloads of Dubuque fans, plus those that drove up on their own, hoping to witness the last game of the playoffs. Added to that was an assortment of parents, family and friends of Minnesota born players. It was a full house.

The two teams fought it out tooth and nail through two periods, racking up 9 penalties each. Mel Bailey was thrown out of the game in the first period for leaving the bench to question an official's call. At the start of the third period, the Saints were ahead by one. The teams traded two more goals before Eric Gager of the Mavericks tied the game with less than five minutes remaining.

With a minute and sixteen seconds remaining in regulation time, as time expired on an Austin penalty, Worps got a pass on the right side of the rink just inside the blue line. He let a slapshot go at the top of the circle that beat the Austin goalie, who made 51 previous saves in the game. Worps' game winning goal gave the Saints their second jewel for the season, the Clark Cup.

On the ice the team celebrated with the trophy, taking it on several laps around the rink. Mel even took it for a lap in his street clothes; he had showered and was watching the final period from the stands.

"Come on every one, pick up Mel!" Worps said as he encouraged everyone to carry Mel on their shoulders. They carried Mel off the ice. The fans roared as Mel held up his arms, relishing the moment. It was the first time that Worps had been nice to Mel since high school.

"What the heck were you thinking, Worps?" Bulldog asked in the locker room after the celebration.

Inside The Locker Room

"I don't think anyone realized that I wasn't being serious. They all started picking him up. I had to go with it after that," replied Worps

In the locker room the guys drank champagne and beer. The celebration lasted for over an hour. The players left and visited briefly with family and friends that were present while Jim Denman drove Worps to the hospital to get stitches. Worps took a stick to the face in the second period.

In the locker room there was debate on whether to split up the team to travel back to Dubuque in the busses with the fans or stick together as a team. There was an obligation to celebrate with the fans, but this was also the last chance to celebrate as a team. The debate was spirited until Jack walked in. "The decision's been made. Players on the team bus; fans on the fan busses," Jack said, ending the debate. "The fans left you guys a surprise on the bus," he added.

When the players got on the bus there was a 30-gallon garbage bin filled with beer and ice in the middle of the aisle. They had to crawl over it to get to the toilet, but that was a simple inconvenience they were willing to put up with. Jack said the fans paid for the beer, but the guys guessed that Doc Field footed the bill. Regardless, they had lots of beer for the ride home. As an added bonus they had a place to put the empties so they didn't roll around on the floor when they got close to Dubuque.

On the bus they took pictures with the Clark Cup. In 1981 the Clark Cup was small, about the size of a large bouquet of flowers, not like the Anderson Cup, which needed to be wheeled around on a cart. Jack joined in the celebration. They told stories and sang songs. They changed the words to their regular song:

In the good ol' wintertime, in the good ol' wintertime,

Skating on Mankato ice, on a forward line.

186

Worps shoots the puck,

He scores a goal,

And that's a really good time.

We just WON the USHL in the good ol' wintertime!

"What's up Worps?" Gibby asked. Worps looked bummed out.

"Nothing really. I just scored the game-winning goal, but it feels like my hockey career is ending. You guys will be going on to college, and I will just be going home," Worps replied honestly. It was one of the few times he was being serious.

"Hey, it's better to end your career by scoring the game winning goal than to end it in the penalty box like I did. Treasure it man, you're a hero," said Gibby, letting it sink in before adding, "Come on, let's have some fun."

After an hour on the road, the party died down and the guys were telling stories and jokes. Gibby was in a group with a few teammates as Jack walked up. Without warning Jack slapped Gibby across the face. It was a hard smack. Gibby grabbed his chin to make sure he still had all his teeth, then grabbed Jack by his sweat suit and reared his arm back to throw a punch.

"Go ahead Gibby, punch me. Go ahead!" Jack said through clenched teeth with his arms at his side seemingly giving Gibby a free shot. This made Gibby stop and think about what he was doing.

"What was that for?" Gibby yelled at Jack still holding him by the collar, wanting to punch the only real coach he had in his short hockey career. The bus was now silent for what seemed like an eternity.

Jack broke the silence, "Go ahead, Gibby, hit me" he repeated.

Gibby was gritting his teeth, still trying figure out why he got slapped. He noticed others on the bus watching. He couldn't punch his coach. He let Jack go and put his hand back to his cheek to see if there would be any permanent damage. That slap felt harder than any punch he received in two years of USHL hockey fights, a lot worse than Murphy's shot to the forehead in tryouts the year before.

Jack waited for Gibby to back down before he hinted at what this was all about. "If you ever talk about my family like that again I'll hit you harder," Jack said.

It was starting to make sense. Gibby couldn't remember exactly what he said, but he knew he made some off-color jokes that Jack took exception to. "I guess I deserved it," Gibby thought to himself, "but man, he didn't have to loosen my teeth!"

Gibby approached Jack and apologized. Jack told Gibby he didn't think he hit him that hard. Gibby took that as an apology. With the incident behind them, the celebration continued, though slightly subdued for Gibby and Worps. They sat in the back of the bus sipping beer and trying to fall asleep.

Nothing could over shadow the accomplishments of this squad of misfit overachievers. Throughout the season they learned that as a team they could play well beyond their preconceived individual limits. They found that success came from every player at the precise time it was needed. The role players rose to the occasion by being in the right place at the right time, with the right skill set to succeed.

Most of their success could be attributed to the coach, and he deserves a lot of the credit; but there was something else that is very rare. These guys were all very different people from different parts of the country; but when they entered the locker room, their differences vanished. A bond was formed that helped the team achieve record book success, in addition to individual growth, proving that the whole is greater than the sum of the individuals.

Throughout the season they also learned important life lessons from Jack, not by enforcing strict rules of behavior, but by allowing them the freedom to make mistakes. These nineteen young athletes had the intestinal fortitude to work properly towards team success combined with the individual moral character to hold themselves in check when success and recognitions came to the forefront. Herb Brooks was prophetic when he told them to "keep it all in the proper perspective."

This group of individuals had now achieved the two main objectives that went unmentioned at the start of the season, The Anderson Cup and the Clark Cup. The only thing left was the National Championship.

Players hold the Clark Cup on the bus after the victory in Mankato, MN.
Front row (left to right): Guy, Vogy, Badger, and Gibby.
Second row: Scanny, Bucky, Nordsy, Dinap Third row: Bulldog, Jask.
Top row: Collins, Mel, TD, Worps (after stitches).

Chapter 6: National Championship

Early in the morning on April 4th, the guys arrived back in Dubuque with another coveted trophy, and a decent hangover. This time there would be no time for extended celebrations. There were only five days until the National Tournament, which began on April 9th.

They would not get another chance to practice on home ice because the Five Flags staff turned off the compressors when they heard that the Saints won the Clark Cup. Their home ice melted away while they slept. The Five Flags staff was busy cleaning up the concrete floor in the late morning when they woke up. Jack decided they needed one more practice before heading to Green Bay for the tournament, so he rented the closest ice available, in Janesville, Wisconsin. The players traveled separately to Janesville in cars, trucks and vans.

"This is stupid. We spend four hours driving for one hour of practice," complained Worps, as he got dressed.

"You're just pissed cuz you're missing your soaps," Gibby replied.

They did a few stretching exercises while waiting for Jack to come out and lead the practice. Jack always came out onto the ice late. Reegs was in his regular jovial mood and playing tricks on his teammates. As they were standing around, Reegs knelt down behind Mel. This was the opportunity for Worps to push Mel over Reegs. He gave Mel a shove, which sent him toppling over Reegs. Reegs got up and laughed as he skated away.

Mel got up and skated over to Worps. "I've had it with your bullshit! I'm sick of it!" Mel screamed in Worps' face. After two seasons of countless sarcasm and ruthless degrading, Mel finally boiled over. Spit was flying from his mouth, his face turning beet red. Worps seriously believed Mel was going to kick his ass. Worps always knew Mel could beat the crap out of him but he wasn't going to back down. He stood his ground while Mel was screaming in his face.

"It was Reegs idea. Why don't you go beat the shit out of him?" Gibby said to Mel, trying to keep the peace in a strange way.

"I don't care. He's been bugging me all year and I'm sick of it!" Mel said. After several tense seconds, Mel skated away mumbling to himself, still red-faced with anger. A physical altercation could have crippled team unity heading into what was possibly the biggest tournament of their lives. Thankfully, the situation was defused when Jack came out onto the ice.

They went through some light drills with very little intensity, passed a few pucks around and took some soft shots on the goalies. "You were right, Worps. This was stupid," said Gibby.

Jack's goal was to do some skating drills and shoot a few pucks to keep their edge; it didn't have to be a full-fledged workout. It would have been hard to be at the top of your game after going six days without being on the ice. After the so-called practice, they headed back to Dubuque. Most of the guys had quit working their day jobs when the playoffs started. They were making plans to leave Dubuque. Some were going to come back to Dubuque after the national tournament, but most were planning to go home directly from Green Bay. There was no team bus to take the players to Green Bay. They were transported in a variety of vehicles driven by Jack, Doc Field and others.

Mel and Gibby loaded up their cars and went back to Minnesota, before making their own way to Green Bay separately. Gibby offered to put Mel's Datsun in the trunk of the big red "Boat." Mel declined the offer saying that his little hot-rod was safer.

The day before the first scheduled game, they all arrived at the cheapest run down fleabag motel in the Green Bay area. The only good thing about it was that it was within walking distance to the Brown County Arena, site of the National Tournament, and Lambeau Field, where the NFL Packers play. They had another slow paced practice then hung around to take fake action pictures on the ice. Gibby took pictures of Vogy hip checking Reegs, attempting to get shots of him flying through the air. He also got still action shots of Jask pretending to make saves.

"Jask, take a picture of Reegs and me in a fight," said Gibby. "Reegs, let's pose in the Doc Field fight, I get to be Doc Field," Gibby stated. Reegs reluctantly agreed to be the guy who gets punched. They did a re-enactment of the famous Toronto newspaper picture of Doc Field grabbing a guy by the face in a fight.

Eventually they got kicked off the ice because the Austin Mavericks were getting set to play the Park Ridge Hornets in a play-in game. The winner would play the Saints in the opening game of the tournament.

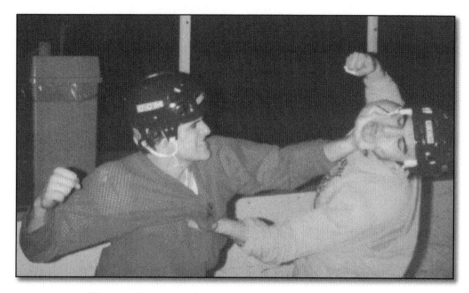

Gibby and Reegs in a remake of the Doc Field fight photo.

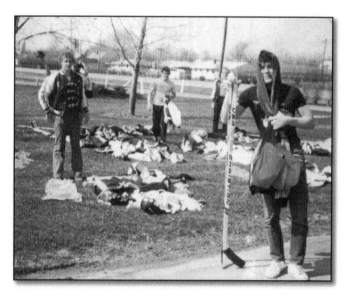

Drying out their gear at the Fleabag Motel: Nordsy, Gibby, Mel, Worps.

April 9th, 1981:

Pool A, Game 1

Game 1: Saints 4, Austin 2

"Saints score early in ousting Mavericks" -*Telegraph Herald*

"Oh great, we get to play the Mad-Dicks again," said Worps when Austin beat the Hornets 6-3. They were getting tired of playing Austin. In twelve matches against the Mavericks this season, the Saints were 8-2-1. This includes their only playoff loss.

The next morning they slept late, went for a short jog and did some calisthenics to get the blood flow going. Then it was a long wait until puck drop at 8 p.m.

It took all of 21 seconds for the Saints to score the first goal, when the first game of the tournament finally got underway. They led by three goals for most of the game. It ended 4-2, and the Austin Mavericks were eliminated from the tournament.

April 10th, 1981:

Pool A, Game 2

Saints 5, Redford 3

"Saints survive tacky tactics of Redford" -Telegraph Herald

The next day the Saints would play the Redford Royals. Both teams were moving on to the semifinals, but this game would determine the seeding. The Saints wanted the number one seed and they didn't like losing.

The Michigan teams were required to wear facemasks. Jack and the players knew it would get physical. The Saints kept their cool as Redford received 26 minutes in penalties to the Saints 12. The action was a near replica of the Austin game. The Saints jumped out ahead early and lead by two for most of the game. Redford's Kelly Miller got them to within one goal with 8 minutes left, but two minutes later Vogy drove home a slapper for the final score and a five to three victory, clinching the top seed in the semifinal.

By now things were getting serious. It was win or go home. After gaining a berth in the finals, Jack imposed a strict curfew. He didn't want anyone staying out too late after this big win, but Jack didn't always get what he wanted.

"Where the hell is he?" Scanny said to Deano in their fleabag hotel room. He was talking about Collins. It was 20 minutes past curfew and Collins was nowhere to be seen. The look of concern was visible on Scanny's face in the dimly lit room.

"I think he went out to have a beer with some friends from Chicago. He'll be fine," Deano tried to reassure Scanny.

"What if Jack comes to check on us?" said Scanny.

"Turn off the lights, maybe he'll pass us by," Deano said.

That didn't work the last time, and it won't work again," Scanny doubted as he turned off the lights.

Five minutes later Jack opened the door slowly and turned on the light. Jack saw that Collins was missing but didn't wake the others from their fake sleep. He walked over to the desk, grabbed a pen and paper and wrote a note to Collins, placing it on his pillow. Jack turned off the light on his way out, never saying a word to the other guys in the room.

Collins strolled into the room about an hour later without turning on the light. He quietly got undressed and slid into bed. When he laid his head down on the pillow, he felt the note against the side of his face. He got back up, walked over to the door and turned on the light to read the note.

"I hope you enjoy the game from the stands.

-Love, Big Daddy"

The other guys in the room groaned at having a light shine in their eyes, but Collins didn't notice. For the first time all season, his trademark grin was absent from his face. This time he was audibly laughing out loud. He turned out the light and went back to bed knowing he would get a good night sleep. He knew Jack wouldn't keep him out of the biggest game of the year.

April 11th, 1981: Semi-Final

Saints 6, Paddock Pools 5, 2OT

"Fighting Saints reach national junior final!" -Telegraph Herald

In the first game against Austin, the stands were mostly empty. It was a Thursday night, and most people had to work. Friday was the same situation. But now, on Saturday, the Dubuque fans were arriving in droves along with a good number of the players' parents and families. Worps' mother and brother drove all the way from Las Vegas.

There were a lot of college and pro scouts in attendance as well. Before the game, Bulldog accepted a full scholarship to play for...yes, you guessed it, the UMD Bulldogs. Earlier in the day, Bulldog was hanging out with his family. He let his niece paint his fingernails. When it came time to sign his official letter of intent, he picked up the pen and signed with pink fingernails.

Chris Guy received an offer from Lake Superior State College, and Jimmy Grillo officially signed his letter to play at Western Michigan. Brian Collins caught up to Bulldog in goals during the playoffs and possessed the size and skill to play at any Division I college; but like Worps, Collins did not see himself going to college. He was willing to take the longer route through the minor leagues.

They would be playing another team from Michigan, the Paddock Pools Saints. They had basically the same logo as the Dubuque Fighting Saints, a winged hockey player with a bamboo halo. The only difference was the

Paddock colors were red and gold. Dubuque was blue and white. The Paddock team also wore facemasks, which meant there would be lots of penalties.

Most people don't remember that in 1980 Team USA's "Miracle On Ice" victory over the Russians was a semifinal game. Team USA had to win one more game for the gold medal. This game for the Saints had a similar feel to the USA-Russia Olympic game. Not because the Saints were underdogs, in fact they were very even teams with similar records in the regular season. It was because the Saints trailed by three goals twice in the second period. The players knew that if they could find a way to win this game, they would be heavy favorites in the championship game.

The Saints scored the first goal but found themselves down 4-1 early in the second period, after Granger was injured by a crosscheck. Jasken replaced Granger and Collins brought the Saints to within two, but the Paddock team answered a minute later. The saving grace was DiNapoli's late second period goal to bring them back to within two goals going into the third.

The Saints wasted little time evening up the score. Deano slammed one in less than a minute into the third, and two minutes later Bulldog tied the game with a backhand off a rebound at the left side of the net. From then on it was back and forth action with the goaltenders being the heroes and sending the game into sudden death overtime.

There were three penalties in the first overtime, two on Paddock and one on the Saints, but still no goals. After the first overtime Doc Field came into the locker room during the intermission and put a hundred dollar bill on the floor in the middle of the locker room. "This is for the guy who scores the next goal," he stated, then he walked out.

Three minutes into the second overtime, the Bulldog line ended the game in what is simply referred to now as "The Goal." The play started just inside the Saints defending blue line with a backhand pass from Chris Guy to his defensive partner Bucky. Bucky then passed the puck up the boards to Deano. Deano passed the puck to Bulldog in the center of the ice. Bulldog took a few strides then handed off the puck to Collins streaking down the right side. Collins drew the goalie and the defensemen over his way at the bottom of the right circle then slipped a beautiful pass between the defenseman's legs back to Bulldog. Standing in the slot with nothing but a wide-open six-by-four net to shoot at, Bulldog scored the "The Goal."

The place erupted and the bench cleared. The jubilation was greater than both the Anderson Cup and Clark Cup celebrations combined. Back in the locker room, the team was ecstatic but drained. It was a battle the likes of which the players had never experienced before. "The Goal" was a fitting way for it to end.

In the locker room after the game, Bulldog returned the hundred-dollar bill to Doc Field. "The Goal was a team effort," he told him.

Doc Field said, "I suppose you're right." It was just like the whole season. It was a team effort from the coach, the players, the front office and the box office. From Betty Wieland and TD Feldman to the DCYHA board and the entire fan base, it was a team effort. Now they had one more game. Win or lose they had only one more game.

April 12th, 1981: National Championship Game

Saints 7, Redford 3

"Saints add final jewel to a sparkling season" -*Telegraph Herald*

Playing in a National Championship game is like nothing else. Knowing that you are playing in your last game of a long season brings out some of the most uniquely bizarre emotions an athlete can experience. You normally don't have much time to think about it because you just earned the right to play the game the night before. The thought of losing never enters your mind. You are too busy getting ready to play the game of your life.

Sometimes you win and the feeling of being on top of the world is overpowering and amazing. It is something that all athletes strive for, thus they make it their ultimate goal. Sometimes you lose and you become physically and emotionally drained. You feel like nothing else could be worse. Few real athletes find solace in second place.

Most of the people who supported the Saints from the beginning were at the game: people like Tom Hill, Doug Jass, Jim Denman and the others that helped create the team; people like Doc Field and the rest of the original investors who never envisioned this type of success in their first year; people like Al Stoltz and Mike Waddick who just wanted to be part of the action.

Finally, the hometown fans travelled to Green Bay by the hundreds, men and women, young and old, couples and whole families. Richard Leonhardt traveled with a group of Saints enthusiasts for the championship game on Sunday but had to go back to work Monday morning. They wouldn't get home until well past 2 a.m. These regular fans bought season tickets or paid each night during the season, searching only for some good entertainment and quality hockey. They were all emotionally invested in a positive outcome.

The game was set for 7:30 p.m. on Sunday April 20, 1981. It would be a rematch of the second Pool A game between the Saints and the Redford Royals of Michigan. Redford beat the Green Bay Bobcats in their semifinal by a score of 5-3.

During a luncheon gathering on the day of the game Jack made a proclamation to the gathering of Dubuque faithful. "I guarantee you; we will not disappoint," he said. His proclamation was premature.

The Saints scored the first goal just 16 seconds into the game on a pass that deflected off a Royal skate from 30 feet out. But the Royals struck back 10 seconds later on a shot that trickled over Jask's pad. They traded power play goals midway through the period, then the Royals took the lead with less than a minute left on a shot from just inside the blue line that bounced off Jask's glove. It was sloppy hockey on both sides. The Saints were letting the season slip away.

"At that point, I knew I had to get myself more into the game. If I can just keep us close," Jask thought to himself. That is exactly what he did. The Royals would not score again.

The Royals held the lead until the later part of the second period when Badger picked up a failed clearing attempt and took a soft shot from the left side that bounced off the goalie's midsection, under his arm and into the net. The score was tied going into the third.

The Royals managed to hold the Bulldog line to only one point, but the rest of the Saints team picked up the slack. The Saints came to life in the third period, finally making Jack's luncheon proclamation come true. Nordsy and Gibby set up Reegs in the slot just 16 seconds in. Reegs fired the puck along the ice into the left side of the net. Badger scored his second of the game three minutes later, then DiNap took over from there. He came into the zone by himself with two defenders to beat. He cut across the high slot and let quick wrister go that froze the goalie and found the upper right corner. He later set up Chris Guy with a beautiful pass that left him nothing but net to shoot at. At the buzzer the Saints piled on Jask and the final on-ice celebration began.

The trophy for winning the national championship paled in comparison to the Anderson and Clark Cups. It looked like a trophy you would win at a weekend PeeWee tournament. Not to be deterred, the players skated laps with it anyway. It was the final jewel in a sparkling season.

In the stands the fans went wild. The celebrations would last well into the next morning. The players met up with family, friends and fans after the game and split up to have dinner and continue the celebration. Parties broke out all around the cheap motel in addition to the hotels the fans stayed in.

Late into the night the cops were called in to quiet things down. It was a Sunday night after all, but the partiers just moved to different locations. Some fans ran out of beer and joined up with a bunch of women from a hairdresser's convention that had a large supply of wine.

It was a great way to end a season that was never expected to be such a success. Jack kept a low profile throughout the celebration because he still had responsibilities. He knew that if the players or fans wanted to get into trouble, there was little he could do to stop them.

Jack went to his hotel room and called Kathy who was back in Dubuque with the kids. "What am I going to do next year?" he asked. Kathy knew exactly what he would do even if he pretended he didn't. In a month he would be back in his office at the Five Flags Center calling his connections to get new players. He would be talking to his counter parts in the USHL to make the league bigger and better than it has ever been. Kathy knew that the game of hockey was in his blood. She knew it was his first passion.

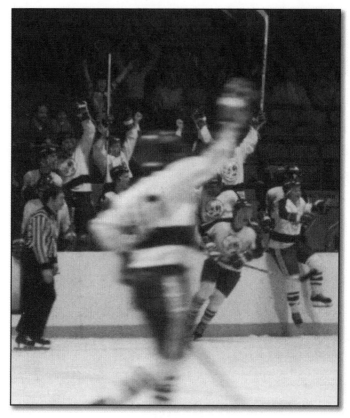

Walshy holds up an arm as the celebration begins.

Chapter 7: Going Home

April 1981

Hockey in the Sun. That is what they called the national broadcast of the championship game on cable TV. The reason for this was that the winning team would earn the right to play the Canadian Junior A champion in Jacksonville, Florida in May. Jack said he would let everyone know when the final date was solidified. Shortly after the game it was announced that the international "Hockey in the Sun" series would be postponed until the following season. This group of players won the right to represent the country and Dubuque versus the Canadians in a mini tournament, but it was next year's team that would reap the benefits. The 81-82 Saints went to Jacksonville and got clobbered by the Canadians. They also got treated like dirt. Doc Field walked out of the banquet with a contingent of prominent hockey representatives from Dubuque, while Ted Lindsay was giving a speech. The tournament became a fiasco; it was also cold, cloudy and rained most of the time they were there. So much for Hockey in the Sun!

The season was over for most of the players when Jack announced that Hockey in the Sun was postponed. Six of the Saints were selected to play in Switzerland as USHL all-stars (Bulldog, Collins, Grillo, Reegs, Vogy, and Mel).

They would be leaving out of Chicago in less than a week. The day after the game, Grillo went home to Hibbing, Minnesota with his family. Mel also went home to Rosemount to be with his family and girlfriend. Bulldog and Vogy went to Chicago with Deano and Collins. They all rode comfortably in a Chevrolet Suburban driven by Deano's dad.

Granger and Walshy went back to Dubuque. Walshy worked at the shoe store for the rest of the month, and then he would head back to the Twin Cities for the summer. Granger stayed in Dubuque to have his shoulder operated on by Doc Field. Jask and Badger went back to Dubuque, where they stayed all summer after getting fulltime jobs.

The two high school boys, Nordsy and Fallon, flew back to their respective homes in Colorado and New York, where they would finish their high school education.

Bucky, Scanny and DiNap loaded up the Datsun B210 and headed out on the long journey to the East Coast. They decided to take the shorter route through Canada. Hopefully, they could get through customs in Sioux St. Marie quickly and be on their way.

DiNap had reservations about going through Canada, but he was out-voted. As they approached the border, DiNap began cleaning up the area in back seat. Being the responsible one he feared that a messy vehicle gave them a better chance of being searched.

"What the heck is this?" he demanded. He held up a sandwich bag with two marijuana joints inside. None of the players smoked pot during the season. If they did it was extremely well hidden and no one talked about it. Now they were about to go through customs with a "baggie" that could land them in jail.

DiNap rolled down the window to throw it out. "Wait! Just hide it good. We'll be fine," came from the front seat. Reluctantly, DiNap hurried to find a good enough hiding place. He stuffed it between the seats.

"That will be the first place they'll look, you idiot," came from the front seat. DiNap was experienced and educated; but in the field of hiding criminal evidence, he was a novice.

"You asshole, you take care of it! I don't want any part of it," he replied and threw the baggie up front.

"Can you reach in my hockey bag and pull out one of the old skates?" asked one of the front seat occupants. When the skate was handed to the front of the car, they were getting closer to customs. The skate had the old type of metal blades that had a white plastic knob on the end. They took a screwdriver, removed the knob, inserted the joints into the skate blade and returned the knob to its original position. "Put it back in my hockey bag."

As they went through customs the agents pulled them aside for a thorough search. Apparently, DiNap was right about the messy car. They pulled the newly crowned national champions out of the car, patted them down, and then proceeded to strip search the entire vehicle and all of its contents. The guys somehow avoided a full body cavity search. The customs agents never pulled the knob off the skate. The three would-be criminals were released into Canada with the contraband. Coming back into the States they breezed through customs. Luck was on their side. DiNap breathed a sigh of relief. No one has publicly claimed ownership of the contraband.

Worps invited Gibby to come to Las Vegas for the summer. They loaded four people and all their bags into the Worpell Mustang Gaia, a smaller 1970's economical version of a regular Ford Mustang. Worps' mom and his brother, Gerard, were in the front seat. Worps and Gibby were in the back seat for the two-day drive.

The plan was for Gibby and Worps to find part time jobs during the summer. Gibby never had a plan for getting back to Minnesota. He also never actually looked for a job. Within a month he was out of money and had to borrow some from a friend of Worps for a plane ticket to Chicago. He got a ride from Deano and his dad from Chicago to Rockford, where he hitchhiked back to Dubuque. He spent a couple weeks there before hitchhiking home to White Bear Lake, Minnesota, where the family planned a welcome home celebration. When he arrived the only thing left of the celebration was a welcome home sign. Too much time had passed, and the family moved on to other summertime activities.

Back in Dubuque the city and townspeople were not finished celebrating. They held one more informal event at the Five Flags Center, which they called the "Victory Celebration."

With all the trophies on display, the night kicked off with Mayor Mike King bestowing Honorary Citizenship certificates to all the players, trainer and coach. Reegs, Mel, Walshy and Badger were in attendance to accept the certificates on behalf of their teammates.

Tom Hill, one of the people who got it all started, stepped up to the microphone. He thanked Jack and the team for their contribution to the Dubuque youth hockey program but reminded them that they were not perfect. "After all, they did lose 9 regular season and one playoff game. That will be the bar for all the teams that follow," he said.

August 1ˢᵗ, 2008:

Motzko Family Home, St. Cloud, MN

"The view from up here is totally awesome," said Worps as he cracked open another beer. Worps and Badger were sitting in recliners looking out over the Las Vegas mountain range from the top floor suite at the five-star hotel. The suite had a full size indoor swimming pool. They sat in silence enjoying the view and the taste of their domestic beer. Their girlfriends were splashing around in the pool behind them, making a lot of noise but they hardly noticed.

Just then Gibby burst into the room with his girlfriend. He left her by the pool and walked over to Worps and Badger.

"Check out the view!" said Worps.

Gibby moved the third recliner closer to his good friends, grabbed a cold beer from the ice filled cooler and kicked up the footrest. "Man this is great," he said as he looked out over the vastness of Nevada.

"I love Vegas," said Worps. "I don't think I'll ever leave here again." The three nineteen-year-old men were at the top of the world. They had just won the National Championship. Nothing could get any better than this.

Worps finished another beer and threw the can out the window, but something went terribly wrong. There was no window. The whole wall was one giant thirty-foot pane of glass. The beer can hit the glass, shaking loose the entire windowpane. The glass wall fell fully intact towards the pedestrian filled pavement three hundred feet below. When it hit the ground it made horrible crashing sound that shook Gibby awake. It was all just a dream.

Gibby still felt like he was in Las Vegas, as he rubbed the light sleep from his eyes. When he was fully awake, he realized he was not in Las Vegas but in Badger's basement in St. Cloud, Minnesota. The three men, nearly fifty years old now, met the night before to have dinner and to relive old stories before heading to Dubuque in the morning. It was to be the first Saints' reunion since winning the National Championship in April of 1981.

Most of Gibby's dreams were nightmares. In most of them he had one game left to play and couldn't make it to the arena, or if he made to the arena he would be mortified to find out that he forgot his skates. In all of his past nightmares, the games would start without him. He would wake up in a cold sweat.

His wife concluded that he had some mental issues and stopped listening to the stories decades ago. She once mentioned that he should get the nightmares interpreted to find out what was causing his deep inner pain, but he never did.

This Vegas dream was different though. The three young men were done with hockey, and the feeling of finishing on top was euphoric. Gibby never told his two teammates about the dream, concluding that they would think he was "mental" like his wife said. Worps' wife, Teri, was there and Badger's wife and three kids were also home. They would only make fun of him.

After a generous breakfast with the Motzko family, Worps asked Gibby about the National Championship rings he was wearing. Gibby had his 81' Saints ring on as well as one from Bemidji State University, where he played hockey in college.

"What about your rings, Badge? You must have a bunch of them," Gibby said, deflecting the attention to Badger.

"They're in my closet in a box," replied Badger seemingly uninterested.

"Go get them. Let's have look," said Worps.

Badger brought out a cigar box filled with huge gold rings with expensive rubies and diamonds, eight or nine of them altogether. Badger explained how he earned each one in his long coaching career.

"Wow! Which one is your favorite?" asked Worps.

Badger pushed the gaudy expensive ones aside and picked out the smallest one; a cheap silver ring that said: "Fighting Saints, 80-81, USA Junior "A" Champions."

Badger held it up in the air. "This is the one. I was a player. I was part of something special."

What a special season it was.

Epilogue

The Brainerd Warriors were playing the Roseau Rams in an important Minnesota State High School League Section 8 game. There were several prominent players being watched by the scouts. One of the players was Aaron Ness from Roseau. He was a junior and the scouts wanted to see what type of magic he created on the ice.

In the first five minutes of the game, Ness got a penalty for hooking. Several minutes later he got another for holding. Jack Barzee, now into his tenth year as an NHL scout, had enough. In between periods he made his way down to the referee's locker room to give the referee a piece of his mind. During his years of coaching, Barzee rarely voiced his displeasure with bad calls by the referees. Now he was an NHL scout, there was nothing holding him back. He thought one of the refs was making some questionable calls. It was time to speak out.

He walked into the locker room as the refs were talking. He rudely interrupted them, "Jesus Christ, Gibby, I came all the way here to watch Ness play, not to see him sit in the damn penalty box!" he said.

"Jack!" Gibby exclaimed loudly. He walked up to his former coach and gave him a hearty handshake and a big sweaty man hug. The smile on his face clearly showed he appreciated the interruption by this man he had not seen in more than a decade. This is the same guy who almost knocked out his molars with a heavy handed slap almost twenty-five years prior. "Man, it's great to see you!" Gibby said, ignoring the white haired man's comments for the time being.

Jack Barzee lost his moniker as the Silver Fox when he stopped coaching in 1986. His hair has turned totally white now in his mid sixties.

"Tell that punk to stop committing fouls, and I'll stop calling penalties," Gibby finally responded, after releasing the tight hug on his former coach and mentor.

The Dubuque Fighting Saints 1980-81 season stands out as one of those unique seasons that defy the odds and created a lifelong bond between the players. Former teammates are now referred to as brothers. Jack Barzee is now their friend and remains their mentor.

There have been two official reunions since 1981. In addition, many of the guys get together when possible to retell stories and catch up on each other's lives. The eastern players had their own impromptu reunion several years ago; and whenever one of the guys is in Las Vegas, they try to hook up with Worps.

The original Dubuque Fighting Saint players have gone on to accomplish a variety of things in their lives, each with their own successes, failures and unique stories to tell. Hopefully, the stories in this book showed the type of people that came together for that one great and glorious season that created the Dubuque Fighting Saints legacy.

Mystique Community Ice Center:

The Mystique Community Ice Center is a beautiful complex located close to the Mississippi River and within walking distance of a huge casino hotel. The inside of the arena has the look and feel of a modern Division I college hockey arena. Modern seating wraps around the entire ice surface, which makes every seat perfect for watching a game. The complex also has a VIP lounge that provides buffet meals and has a full service bar.

At the top of the stairway entrance to the open arena, is the Dubuque Fighting Saints Main Office. They have seven full time staff working especially hard on game days, preparing for the influx of loyal Saints fans. Every detail is arranged to make the games a pleasurable experience for the whole family, with various promotions and fun activities in addition to the quality hockey on the ice.

Underneath the seats is a spacious locker room complete with a large Saints logo on the red carpet and modern technology to review game videos and draw up strategies. The athletes have an attached weight and exercise room, with all the devices needed to stay at peak physical condition during the season.

The current organization has a three-man coaching staff, in addition to a strength and conditioning coach, an athletic trainer and an equipment manager. They also have a long list of scouts and player personnel to recruit top-notch hockey talent, from around the country and the world. The USHL now allows three foreign-born players per team.

But the Mystique Community Ice Center is not just about the Saints. All levels of the youth program practice and play games at the arena. The adult league also maintains a full schedule. The ice surface is rarely vacant during the winter, making the Mystique Community Ice Center one of the most popular facilities in Dubuque since it replaced the Five Flags Center in 2010 as the only indoor ice surface.

Ever since the Saints were created in 1980, hockey fans in Dubuque have expected a winning season. In that first year the Saints went 50-10-1, on their way to the National Championship. Two years later they did it again with an almost exact record. From 1986 to 2001, after the departure of Coach/General Manager Jack Barzee, the team struggled to win and attendance dropped. In 2001 the team changed its name and moved to Tulsa Oklahoma, in an effort to repeat the inaugural success of the Saints. The move failed to generate any excitement, and the organization folded after one season.

To fill the void left by the Saints departure, the Dubuque Thunderbirds were created by local hockey enthusiasts. The Thunderbirds competed at the Junior A Tier III level in the CSHL (Central States Hockey League) and enjoyed great success, winning 4 League titles in nine years and smashing CSHL attendance records, with crowds at the Five Flags Center equaling that of the Saints initial season.

In 2009 the city of Dubuque built the 3079-seat Mystique Community Ice Center. The following winter the Dubuque Fighting Saints were back in the USHL. Once again the team created excitement in the community as Brooks Bertsch, a Dubuque native, scored the team's first USHL goal in a decade. Success returned on the ice by winning the USHL Clark Cup. In the stands attendance averaged close to 2500 fans per game. In 2013 the Saints won the regular season championship and the Anderson Cup made its way back home to Dubuque for the first time in 30 years. They also won the Clark Cup for the second time in three seasons. Since the Saints reemergence in the USHL, the premier Junior A league in the country, they have qualified for the playoffs in a record 8 straight seasons.

With the tradition of hockey success in Dubuque, it's no wonder the fans expect a winner. However, goals and victories are hard to come by in the USHL today. Current USHL players are fast and move the puck faster. Goalies take up much more of the net with larger more modern equipment, and the play is forced to the sides of the rink by solid defense up the middle. Double digit scoring is almost unheard of today.

It wasn't always this way. In a two-week span in November of 1980, the Dubuque Fighting Saints beat the Waterloo Black Hawks 11 to 7; then beat St. Paul 10-8; then Waterloo again 17-3; and Bloomington 9-2. In fact, the 1980-81 Saints registered double-digit goals in a quarter of all their games. They scored fewer than 4 goals in only 3 games and won all 3 of those. They averaged 7.31 goals per game and 3.89 goals against. The style of play was much more open and the players more "flashy." The modern game is just as physical but probably less physically punishing. In 1980-81 there were "big hit" body checks and regular fights in almost every game, if not every period.

Some of the rules have changed as well as the style of play, but the quality of the players was not that much different. While most of today's USHL players have commitments to Division I colleges, in 1981 there were a lot fewer scholarships available; because there were a lot fewer Division I teams in the country.

The current USHL is producing numerous NHL players, but there were also plenty of future NHL players back then. In the 1980-81 season, there were at least six players that would have long distinguished NHL careers...none of them played for the Saints.

The St. Paul Vulcans had Phil Housley (Buffalo Sabers, 22 years) and Jim Johnson (Pittsburg Penguins, 16 years). Rick Zombo (Detroit Red Wings, 12 years) played for the Austin Mavericks. Bob Mason (Washington Capitals, 8 years and a Stanley Cup Conference Final) played goalie for the Green Bay

Bobcats and is currently the goalie coach for the Minnesota Wild. There was also Kelly Miller (NY Rangers/Washington Capitals, 16 years) who played for the Redford Royals; a team the Saints would beat twice to win the national title, and Tony Granato (LA Kings, a Stanley Cup final and current coach of the University of Wisconsin Badgers) who played for the Elmhurst Huskies.

The 1980-81 Saints may not have had any NHL caliber players, but they knew how to win. They were most likely the strangest bunch of misfit players to ever wear a Fighting Saints jersey; and yet, somehow their unique combination of personalities and talent was the perfect recipe to take the USHL by storm and leave a lasting legacy in the city of Dubuque, on and off the ice.

The current Fighting Saints locker room contains large stalls with nametags, dual shelves, under-seat storage and red carpeting.

Where Are They Now?

Jack Barzee: General Manager/Coach

Residence: Burnsville, MN

Wife: Kathy. Children: Zach, Joel. 5 grandchildren

Jack was the General Manager/Coach and part owner of Dubuque Fighting Saints Tier 1 Jr. A team thru 1985 and Assistant Coach of 1984 Team USA World Junior team. He sold his share in the Dubuque Fighting Saints organization, after getting hired by Central Scouting, the NHL's main scouting organization.

In 1986 the Barzee family moved to Burnsville, MN. He became the Chief USA scout for the Washington Capitals of the NHL from 1989 to 1993, before returning to the Central Scouting organization in 1993. He retired from Central Scouting in 2014.

Currently Jack and Kathy spend most of their time traveling the world and spending time with their kids and grandkids. Jack maintains a close relationship with his former players whenever possible. He and Kathy also stay in touch with the many friends they made in Dubuque. Jack stays active playing golf, and watching his grand kids play hockey.

#1 Brian Granger, Goalie

Born: Bloomington, MN

Current Residence: Eden Prairie, MN

Wife: Chris. Children: Jasper 22, Denali 20, MacKenzie 18, Dawson 16.

Brian required surgery after the shoulder injury in Green Bay. Doc Field performed the surgery in Dubuque. The next year Brian played for Waterloo at the start of the season, while he went to college at Iowa State University. He returned to Dubuque after a month, because the commute to Iowa City was too long. He played most of the second season in Dubuque.

Brian earned a Bachelor of Arts Degree in Business Administration with an emphasis in Accounting and Finance at St. Thomas College in St. Paul, MN. He then used his degree working jobs in Alaska and Seattle from 1986 to 1994, before returning to the Twin Cities. He is currently the director of finance at Ameriprise Financial corporate headquarters in Minneapolis, MN.

#2 Glenn "Bucky" Gilbert, Defense

Born: Northfield, VT

Current Residence: Cape Cod, MA

Wife: Lauri. Children: Matt 30, Ben 27 and Margaret 25. 2 grandchildren.

Bucky returned to Dubuque for the second season in 1981-82 as co-captain, leading the team to a second place finish. After returning home he moved from Vermont to Cape Cod, MA, to play summer hockey and ended up staying there for rest of his life. In 1985 he married his neighbor and coached the local high school hockey team. Bucky got a job in 1987 with a natural gas company as a laborer. Today he serves as a safety and compliance inspector with the same company.

After leaving Dubuque Bucky never went to college and never played competitive hockey. Ironically, both his sons earned college degrees, while playing competitive athletics in baseball and soccer. His daughter is currently earning her master's degree in Psychology.

222

Bucky plays golf, races cars in the super modified category, and enjoys snow skiing with his family.

#3 Mike Fallon, Defense

Born: Long Island, NY

Current Residence: Cazenovia, NY

Wife: Paula. Children: Markus 34, Katherine 31.

Mike Fallon's story since leaving Dubuque is an inspiring tale. While in Dubuque Mike regularly skipped school but somehow graduated back in NY. He was accepted at both Princeton and Brown University. He chose Brown because they recruited him to play hockey.

Mike stayed in touch with his Dubuque girlfriend, Julie Avery. Later in the summer he learned that Julie was undergoing extensive surgery for cancer at the Mayo Clinic in Rochester, MN. He spent 10 days living with Badger in Austin, MN, and visiting Julie at the Mayo Clinic. Mike stayed in close contact with Julie for a year, while he was studying and playing hockey at Brown University. He played in 23 of 26 varsity games at Brown University in his freshman year.

During the next summer Julie's cancer returned, and she passed away on August 27, 1982. In the fall Mike returned to Brown, but his heart was no longer in the game or his studies. Mike was in a state of shock from Julie's passing. He left Brown and returned to Dubuque to play for the Saints.

Early in the season Mike was lethargic and was constantly sick. Finally, on the advice of Jim Denman, he went to a doctor and was diagnosed with stage 3 Hodgkin's disease. He immediately flew home to New York and underwent chemotherapy. Instead of playing hockey he was fighting for his life. After beating the disease and regaining his strength, he went back to Brown the next fall as a junior. The following year the disease returned. Once again he beat it with chemotherapy, but this time the treatment took its toll on his psyche. He told Nordsy that if it returned a third time, he would refuse treatment.

After his college hockey days were over, Mike played hockey professionally in Europe. He played one year in Stockholm, Sweden. In one of his games he took a slap shot in the eye socket that damaged his left eye beyond repair. With only one functioning eye, his dreams of becoming a surgeon were dashed. He currently wears a patch over the damaged eye.

During his final year of Med School, Hodgkin's returned a third time. Staying true to his word, he refused chemotherapy. He took a leave of absence from Med School and changed his diet. Surprisingly, the disease went into remission and has not returned. Mike finished Med School and did his residency in northern Wisconsin, where his met his wife Paula. Eventually, he became a radiologist and oncologist, fighting the disease that nearly took his life.

If ever there is an inspiring story for a book, it would be the life of Mike Fallon; but he is too humble for that, preferring instead to blow it off as something anyone would have done given the same circumstances.

Mike and Paula live in Cazenovia, New York and they both work at Radiation Oncology Services in Cazenovia.

#4 Curt "Vogy" Voegeli, Defense

Born: Cheshire, CT

Current Residence: Cheshire, CT

Wife: Lori. Children: Lindsay 25, Allison 21.

After the national tournament in Green Bay, Vogy played for USHL All-Star team in Switzerland. Vogy attended college in Connecticut in the fall, but it did not last long. His old teammate, Brian Collins, urged him to return to the Midwest to play professionally in the minor leagues. He packed his bags and headed to Peoria, Illinois, to play in the International Hockey League for the Peoria Prancers. Vogy played part of the year in Peoria then was moved to Fort Wayne, Indiana, to play for the Komets.

In December of that season, Vogy and Collin played with the Dubuque Fighting Saints 1981-82 team in Jacksonville, Florida, against the Canadian Junior A champion. He and Collins were over-age players; but this was allowed in the Jacksonville series because the Saints were only playing Canadians.

The following year Vogy decided to put down the hockey stick and pick up a hammer. He began working in the carpentry business. He now owns and operates C. Voegeli Home Improvements, a construction company based in Cheshire, Connecticut.

Vogy met his wife Lori through friends in 1989, and they were married in 1991. Lori is a 4th grade teacher in Cheshire. They have two daughters that both graduated from Penn State. Lindsay is a registered dietitian at the U of Maryland Health Center, and Allison just went to work as an Allocation Analyst at the corporate headquarters of T.J. Maxx in Boston, Mass.

#5 Denny "Gibby" Gibbons, Defense

Born: White Bear Lake, MN

Current Residence: Cohasset, MN

Wife: Marie. Children: Callihan 29, Kassandra 27, Maggie 21.

Gibby committed to play for Bemidji State University in northern Minnesota after being recruited by his brother, Mike. However, after receiving a favorable financial grant to play at St. Thomas College in St. Paul, Gibby stayed in the Twin Cities. He left St. Thomas in early January 1982 and returned to Dubuque to play out the remaining season with the Saints. On the advice of his brother, he returned to Bemidji State. In three years at Bemidji State, Gibby and his team earned three national championship appearances, winning one and runner up twice. In the NCAA II National Championship season, they set a collegiate record for most wins in an undefeated season (31-0, 1984). Combined with the following year, they set another record for the longest winning streak (42 games, 1983-85) in men's college hockey history. Both records stand to this day. In his senior year Gibby was selected to the NCHA All-Conference Team (1985) and NCAA II All-American First Team (1985). He earned a Bachelor of Science Degree in Business Administration, with a Philosophy minor.

Gibby met his wife Marie in 1983 in Bemidji, MN. They were married in 1985 and have three adult children. Marie is a middle school teacher in Grand Rapids, MN. Gibby has worked in the Information Technology field in Grand Rapids, MN since 1991. He has officiated youth and high school hockey games since 1985 and lacrosse since 2010. His hobbies include deer/turkey hunting and golf.

#6 Mel Bailey, Defense

Born: Rosemount, MN

Current Residence: Thailand

All efforts to contact Mel for the writing of this book were unsuccessful. Information on his life since 1981 is sketchy but here is what is known:

After the national tournament in Green Bay, Mel played for the USHL All-Star team in Switzerland. In the 1981-82 season he went to the University of Minnesota Duluth as a walk-on. Mel transferred to Concordia College, Moorhead, MN, in 1982 playing at the Division III level for two more years. Mel earned a Bachelor of Science degree with a double major in Criminology and Political Science.

After graduation from college Mel served his country with distinction in the FBI, engaging in many undercover and regular assignments. Mel took out the "bad guys" throughout his working career, just like he did at the Five Flags

Center in 1980-81. He retired from the FBI in 2012 after 24 years of service. He then moved to Thailand with his wife and children.

#7 Chris Guy, Defense

Born: Littleton, Colorado

Current Residence: Centennial, Colorado

Wife: Julie.   Children: Ryan 28, Shane 25.

After the national tournament in Green Bay, Chris Guy returned to Littleton, Colorado with his family. His dad wanted him to attend the University of Colorado the following year, but Chris had signed a letter of intent to play for Lake Superior State in Sioux St. Marie, Michigan. Chris played four years for the Lakers, amassing 23 goals and 97 assists in 154 games. He currently sits in the thirteenth spot for career assists with the Lakers.

After his freshman season Chris was selected to represent his country playing for the USA World Junior U20 team. On that team Chris played alongside Chris Chelios, Phil Housley, Tom Kurvers, Mark Fusco, Cory Millen and John Vanbiesbrouck, all future American NHL standouts. In his senior year the

232

Lakers made it to the Division I college hockey semifinals before succumbing to RPI, the eventual national champions.

Chris dated his childhood sweetheart in high school; and they stayed together throughout his hockey travels, eventually getting married in the summer of 1984. Julie attended nursing school while Chris was earning his Bachelor of Science degree in Business Administration and Accounting. After college Chris signed to play professionally in the NHL (Netherlands Hockey League). He and Julie spent a year living in Holland.

Chris and Julie now live in Centennial, Colorado, where Chris works as a CFO for Native Rank Digital Marketing. Julie is the Director of Physician Services at a local hospital. When not working Chris enjoys golf and mountain biking.

#8 Glenn "Scanny" Scanlan, Defense/Forward

Born: Lawrenceville, NJ

Current Residence: Mechanicsburg, PA

Wife: Audrey. Children: Emma 30, Bill 28, Harriet 25.

Scanny went to Trinity College in Hartford, Connecticut. He played hockey at the Division III level all fours years of college and earned a Bachelor of Arts degree in History. He earned his master's in education at the University of Connecticut.

In the following years he met a teacher named Audrey, his future wife. They were married in 1984 and started a family. Scanny got a job at an insurance company to pay bills and climbed the corporate ladder. He now works from his home in Mechanicsburg, PA, as an Underwriting Liaison for United Health Care.

While they were raising their family, Audrey had a calling to join the church. Audrey attended Yale Divinity College. She then became a priest in the

Episcopalian church. In 2015 Audrey was elected as a Bishop for the church in the state of Pennsylvania.

#9 Bob "Badger" Motzko, Forward

Born: Austin, MN

Current Residence: Twin Cities, MN

Wife: Shelley. Children: Ella 19, Mack 17, Beau 13.

After the Dubuque season Bob Motzko went to the University of Minnesota as a walk-on and was cut twice in two years. In 1984 he transferred to St. Cloud State University and played for the Huskies for a year at the Division II level. He then decided he wanted to coach. At the start of his senior year, he resigned as a player and took on the role of assistant coach. Bob went back to the USHL as Coach of the North Iowa Huskies. He led the team to the National Championship in his first full year as Coach/General Manager.

Here is a long list of his coaching achievements since 1986:

> 1989 and 2000 USHL General Manager of the Year
> 2006 and 2007 NCAA (WCHA) Coach of the Year
> 2014 NCAA (NCHC) Coach of the Year (Herb Brooks Award), &

Reg. Season Champion

2016 NCAA (NCHC) Champion

2017 U20 WJC Gold Medal

2018 NCAA (NCHC) Coach of the Year (Herb Brooks Award)

2018 NCAA (NCHC) Reg. Season Champion (Penrose Cup)

2018 U20 WJC Bronze Medal

March, 2018 hired by the University of Minnesota as Head Hockey Coach

His former Saints teammates still refer to him as Badger.

#10 Jim "Walshy" Walsh, Forward

Born: Rosemount, MN

Current Residence: Stillwater, MN

Wife: Linda.   Children: Kelli 33, Jenna 28.

Jim returned to Dubuque after the national championship to work at Marting Shoe store. The following season he attended the University of Wisconsin River Falls. He earned a Bachelor of Science degree in Business Management, while playing hockey for the UWRF Falcons. The Falcons won the NAIA Division III National Championship in 1983. His future wife, Linda, was a cheerleader for the Falcons. They were married in 1985 and have two daughters. Jim coached his daughter Jenna through youth hockey and has been an assistant coach for the University of Wisconsin River Falls Women's Hockey team since 2008.

Jim currently works as a Claims Agent for State Farm Insurance in River Falls and enjoys bow hunting in addition to snowmobiling and fishing.

#10 Jimmy "Gringo" Grillo, Forward

Born: Hibbing, MN

Current Residence: Grand Rapids, MN

Wife: Anne.   Children: Alexandra 25, Joey 21.

Jimmy received a full scholarship to the Western Michigan University for hockey. He played 4 seasons with the Broncos. He earned a Bachelor of Science degree in Business Administration and Marketing. He returned to Hibbing, MN, after college working for two years before moving to Chicago as Regional Sales Manager for Trellex, a company in the mining industry. A couple years later he moved back to Minnesota to work for Sensus, Inc. He then reconnected with a girl from Hibbing during the summer. They have been married for 28 years and have two children; Alexandra, 28, who works in Public relations, and Joey, who is a student at the U of M Duluth.

In 2017 Jimmy and Anne moved to Grand Rapids, MN, to enjoy the outdoors. He spends a lot of his summer boating on the lake, and hunting in the fall.

#12 Jeff "Reegs" Regan, Forward

Born: St. Cloud, MN

Current Residence: Ohio

Children: Jillian 33, Olivia 21, Sara 20.

Reegs was a late selection to join the USHL All-Stars in Switzerland after the season ended. From there he went back to Dubuque to spend some time with Tom Hill's daughter, RuthAnn. They dated regularly during the 80-81 Saints season. Reegs went to Western Michigan as a walk-on for the 1981-82 season. The following year they hired a new coach. Reegs knew he was not going to be on the roster so he returned to Dubuque. Reegs married RuthAnn, and they had a daughter, Jillian. In order to provide for his new family, Reegs enlisted in the Army and served three years, a majority of it overseas.

When he returned his marriage was failing. He began working at a group home for mentally challenged adults, in addition to helping his dad with his land surveying business in St. Cloud, MN.

Reegs' brother, Mark, is mentally handicapped, which provided him with the capacity to work part time for Mary T Inc., a group home for mentally challenged adults. Reegs wrote a book about his life based on a man he met at the group home. It is a captivating story about Ken, a down-syndrome man that Reegs helped live and die. It is also a story about how Ken helped Reegs live. The book is called "A Ward of the State" by Jeffery Regan. It was published by Xlibris press in 2009 and is available on Amazon.com.

Reegs spent a majority of his adult life helping his dad with his surveying business. Reegs currently resides in Ohio and works as a land surveyor for Universal Pegasus Gas & Oil Services. His official title at UPG&O is "Party Chief."

#16 Mike "Bulldog" Carlson, Forward

Born: Two Harbors, MN

Current Residence: Greenville, SC

Wife: Roni. Children: Adam 24.

After the national tournament in Green Bay, Bulldog played for the USHL All-Star team in Switzerland. He went to the University of Minnesota Duluth (UMD) playing in two games during the 1982 season. The following year he enrolled at Bemidji State University to play with Gibby but left after only a week. He then went to Warroad, MN, to play for the Warroad Lakers, a senior men's team. In 1984 he went back to UMD and tried out for the team under a new coach. Using his natural talent he scored several goals in try-outs but was cut on the final day. He finished his education at UMD, earning a degree in physical Education with a Health minor. After graduation a friend invited him down to Greenville, South Carolina, where he has remained ever since.

Bulldog is currently a Warehouse Manager for Grainger Companies in Greenville. Bulldog continues to play men's league hockey, now as a defenseman, and restores classic cars in his spare time.

#17 Brian Collins, Forward

Born: Palentine, IL

Current Residence: Gilbert, IL

Wife: Peggy. Daughter: Joey Marie 35. Grandkids: 2 boys

Collins was selected as one of the All-Stars to represent the USHL in Switzerland after the national tournament in Green Bay. The following season he got a try-out with the Peoria Prancers, a professional minor league team in the International Hockey League. He called Vogy and convinced him to drop out of college and give it a try. Both he and Vogy made the team initially but were sent to the Fort Wayne Komets and then to the Danville Dashers in the Continental League. In the meantime both he and Vogy played with the Saints in Jacksonville, Florida. This opportunity came about as a result of the Saints winning the National Tournament the previous year.

At the beginning of his second year in Danville, two guys checked Collins at the same time; one of them hit him low and blew out his knee. He underwent reconstructive surgery but was done for the season. The following season he returned to Danville, but he lost interest about half way through and returned to the Chicago area.

He started working at O'Hare airport in Chicago in 1984 and worked there for 10 years. In 1985 he met Peggy at the airport. They lived together for 10 years before getting married in 1994.

Deano and Brian remain close friends. In 1994 Collins began working as a carpenter. Soon after Deano contracted with Brian to help him with some condominiums he was building. At that point Collins had decided to work for himself and created BC Construction, which he continues to operate today.

Brian and Peggy Collins currently have one daughter and 2 grand-boys. Brian spends most of his time chasing the grandkids. He also plays golf when time allows.

#18 Jon "Nordsy" Nordmark, Forward

Born: Westminster, CO

Current Residence: Highlands Ranch, CO

Wife: Connie. Boys; Quin 15, Tait 9.

Most of Nordsy's family came out to Green Bay to take part in the national tournament. They flew home together from Green Bay. Nordsy had to transfer back to his high school in Westminster, CO, where he finished out the last month and a half of high school.

During the summer Nordsy explored his opportunities to play college hockey. He visited Air Force Academy, but he wanted to play at the Division I level if he could. Bob Johnson at the University of Wisconsin wanted Nordsy to play another year for the Saints, before he would consider him. Nordsy' parents made it clear that if he went back to Dubuque, he would get no financial support. Nordsy finally decided it was best to end his hockey career and start college.

He enrolled at the University of Colorado but missed playing the game he loved. Jack called him on occasion, asking him to come back and play. Nordsy would drive to Dubuque from Denver several times over the next few years to play in Saints games during the weekends then return to Denver without informing his parents.

Nordsy graduated in the top 5% at the U of Colorado with a Bachelor of Science Degree in Business Administration. He worked in marketing for his Dad's company for a short time before deciding to travel to Europe. He spent a summer putting on 3000 miles peddling a bicycle around Great Britain and Northern Ireland with 5 college buddies.

He finally got serious about a job when he started in marketing at Samsonite in 1988, eventually rising to the level of Head of Sales and Marketing in North and South America. In 1998 he quit his high level job at Samsonite to start his own business (eBags) that would sell luggage over this new thing called the Internet. The CEO of Samsonite at the time told Jon "he would never sell a bag through email."

Over ten years eBags grew from one employee to more than 180. As CEO, Nordsy was responsible for revenue of over 103 million a year. Almost all of the revenue came over the Internet, through email. Nordsy eventually stepped down as CEO to become Chairman, while he helped start-up technology companies across the globe. Currently, Nordsy is founder of a company called Iterate. His company can be found on the web at www.iterate.ai.

Nordsy reunited with a girl friend from high school in 2001, and they were married the next year. They have two sons and spend time together traveling the world.

#19 Tod "Worps" Worpell, Forward

Born: Las Vegas, NV

Current Residence: Las Vegas, NV

Wife: Teri.   Children: Stephanie 34, Trevor 29, Beau 24, 3 grandkids.

Worps returned to the Dubuque Fighting Saints for one more year, squeaking in under the age restriction by four days. He returned to the Saints as the Captain of the 81-82 team and led the Saints to a second place finish. He then moved back to Las Vegas, where he made a decent living as a bartender. In 2001, just few months before 9/11, he joined the Las Vegas Fire Department.

Worps drives the fire trucks and mans the ladder/bucket rig. On one of his first calls, Worps lifted fire fighters onto the roof of a burning building. His fire fighter teammates went over to other side of the roof to fight the blaze. Worps watched in horror as the fire quickly spread towards the bucket and the only means of escape for his teammates.

Once a fire fighter team is lifted onto a roof, the standard procedure is not to move the bucket. The reason for this is so the fire fighters know the location of their escape. If the location moved it could create chaos and cost the lives of his crew.

The fire spread over the bucket and Worps watched it burn, fearing that the chances of escape were burning with it. A short time later he was relieved to learn that the crew had escaped down the other side of the roof.

He was reprimanded for letting the bucket burn, but the alternative was not acceptable. It is the kind of thing you would expect from Worps. He would hold his ground for his teammates no matter the cost to him personally. Today, Worps remains one of Las Vegas' Finest and continues to play hockey in the annual "Guns and Hoses" charity hockey game between the Cops and the Fire Fighters.

#20 Dean "Deano" Thomas, Forward

Born: Park Ridge, IL

Current Residence: Grays Lake, IL

Wife: Christi.   Children: Kelsey 32, Courtney 29, Adam 25.

At the end of the season, Deano briefly went back to Illinois, before embarking on what he calls his "Victory Tour." He went back to Dubuque for a few days then rode with Badger to a weekend gathering of Saints players on Gibby's parent's houseboat. From there he visited Bulldog in Two Harbors, then over to Hibbing to play some summer pickup hockey with Grillo. He then returned to Dubuque to have an operation on his shoulder. Throughout most of the 80-81 season; Deano played with a painful shoulder injury that needed to be taped and bandaged to keep him from falling apart.

The following year he attended Iowa State University playing for the Cyclones. The fledgling club program was hoping to move into the Division I college ranks but that never happened. He returned to Miami of Ohio to get a degree in architecture. Throughout this time he continued to date Christy. She worked at University of Cincinnati Hospital as a Respiratory Therapist. In August of 1985 they were married. Deano earned his master degree from the University of Oregon in 1987. Deano owned and operated DGT Designers and Builders Inc. in the Chicago area for about 20 years. His business remains incorporated, but Deano is currently employed by Airoom Architects-Builders as a manager. Christy is an Administration Coordinator for TJ Maxx.

#21 John "Dinap" DiNapoli, Forward

Born: Concord, NH

Current Residence: Sturbridge, MA

Wife: Joy. Children: Nate 28, Kate 28, Heather 28, (triplets!)

After the Saints season DiNap went to New England College to complete his education and play Hockey. DiNap played at New England College for 3 years scoring 69 points in 68 games while leading the Pilgrims to the Eastern Division II quarterfinals in his senior year. He graduated with Bachelor of Arts degree in Business Management. He is currently working as a Manager of Municipal Services at a private gas and electric utility company in Sturbridge, MA.

After his playing days were complete Dinap took to the ice as a referee. He started out officiating high school games then moved to Div. II and III college hockey. He was a linesman in Division I games for 5 of his 16 year career.

As a linesman he was referred to as a Puck Puppy, because he fetched pucks. His fellow referee's told him, "Go get it boy." When he brought it back they said, "drop it."

#30 Mark "Jask" Jasken, Goalie

Born: St. Cloud, MN

Current Residence: Gilbert, AZ

After the national tournament Jask returned to Dubuque to work through the summer. He played goalie for the Saints for most of the 1982-83, before moving to Des Moines. He later moved back to Minnesota. He currently does woodworking and cabinetry. Jask retains the title as "The Keeper of All Knowledge," with regards to the 80-81 season records and statistics. He does not use, or need, a smart phone to look up information. Jask is a walking, talking scrapbook.

Jask currently resides in a suburb of Phoenix, Arizona. Jask enjoys taking evening bike rides after the hot suns sets. On these treks he visits with neighbors and strangers alike.

Trainer Timm "TD" Feldman

Born: Dubuque, IA

TD did not return in his role as part-time trainer for the Saints the following season. He attended Clarke College in Dubuque as a nursing student. Sadly, on July 22, 1986, TD suffered cardiac arrest on his way to Madison, WI, to receive a heart transplant. EMT's restarted his heart, and he was airlifted to UW Madison, where they began the transplant immediately; but he suffered irreversible brain damage during the initial cardiac arrest. TD was 27 years old.

The players recalled what great personality traits TD carried with him throughout his short life. At the first Saints reunion in 2008, a hockey video was created and dedicated in memory of TD Feldman.

Al Stoltz:

Stoltzy was a linesman in the USHL until the Saints first run ended in 1986. He then worked for the Dubuque Thunderbirds. He retired from officiating hockey in 2009. He is now a high school basketball referee and umpires softball and baseball. Al and his wife Lori have 5 kids and 5 grandchildren. Al currently works at Emmaus Bible College and resides in Dubuque.

Mike Waddick:

Waddy officiated in the USHL for ten more years. He graduated from the linesman position and started working as a referee from 1985 to 1990. He took four years off then returned to help with the Dubuque Thunderbirds.

Waddy became Iowa's first USA Hockey (formerly AHAUS) Clinic Instructor in 1986. USA Hockey instituted training on how to break up fights around this time. He continued to officiate hockey at many different levels until 2017.

Waddy currently works for Alliant Energy as Chief Plant Operator. He and his wife, Cathy, raised five boys in Dubuque and now have five grandchildren.

During the 1980-81 season Waddy worked with Jask and Collins at the Dubuque power plant, and they became close friends. "The first Saints season was the most enjoyable of my entire hockey career. I have many fond memories of that season," said Waddy.

Jim Denman Family:

Jim stayed active with the Saints organization. Jim and Ginny Denman sold Oakridge Sports in 2011. Jim started working at a Steamatic franchise in Dubuque in 1993 then purchased it in 1997 as a side business, which has now grown to include two other franchise locations.

Jim and Ginny have since moved to Stone Lake, Wisconsin. Jim now serves as a bartender at Black Bear Pub in Stone Lake, giving advice freely to all who ask and some who don't. Their son, Tony, is now a successful Mortgage Broker in Omaha, Nebraska, after serving his country in the Air Force as an Elite Guard at Strategic Air Command. Not to be out done, Jim and Ginny's other son, Nathan, joined the Navy as a "Top Gun" fighter pilot serving his country with honor for several years, including combat missions in both Iraq and Afghanistan (2001, 2003 and 2007). Nate now serves in the Navy Reserve and works in the options trading field.

Tom Hill:

Tom continues to support the Dubuque Fighting Saints organization as a season ticket holder and one of their biggest fans. Tom worked at John Deere for 27 years, retiring on July 1st, 2000. The Hills had five children (one girl, four boys) and 10 grandchildren. All of the Hill boys played youth hockey in Dubuque; two of them played hockey for the Saints, Dick and Brian. Brian is listed in the USHL's top-ten for career point totals. The Hill family also continues to foster a close relationship with the Barzee family.

Doug Jass:

Doug worked for AT&T. His job was moved to Minneapolis in 1984. He lived there for 4 years before moving to Remer, Minnesota. In 2014, he and his wife, Marilynn, returned to Iowa, settling in the small town of Garner west of Mason City.

Doc Field:

As an orthopedic surgeon, Doctor David Field operated on the shoulders of Brian Granger and Dean Thomas after the season ended. Both former patients of Doc Field were elated with the outcome of their surgeries and returned the following season with full functionality. Doc Field continues to work as an orthopedic surgeon in Dubuque and remains involved with the current Dubuque Fighting Saints organization. In addition to being one of the original Saints investors in 1979, Doc Field also helped to create the new Dubuque Fighting Saints USHL franchise in 2010.

Acknowledgements

On August 17th I took a call from Jack Barzee asking for information about the 1979 Hennepin Nordiques season. I told Jack I would consult my scrapbook for the information he needed. Every day for two weeks I searched for my scrapbook but couldn't find it. For some strange reason, it was then that I decided to write this book. I still haven't found my scrapbook.

As I was searching for my scrapbook, I called Jack and told him of the idea for this book. When I told Jack about idea, he sent me a scrapbook that was meticulously created by Betty Weiland, the secretary during Jack's years in Dubuque. This scrapbook had almost every article written in the Telegraph Herald, during the Saints first season, in addition to clippings of Saints marketing ads, pictures and rosters. There were even newspaper articles from Waterloo, Des Moines and Green Bay. The work Betty did in 1981 laid the foundation for making these stories come together.

Of course, this book would not have been completed without the close help of Jack and Kathy Barzee. They believed in this project and helped all along the way. This book would not have been completed without Jack's continuous calls with additional information. Kathy helped confirm or deny facts that Jack could not recall. She also spent hours reviewing the manuscript for errors.

There were times I was afraid Jack would try to take control of the content and censor some of the stories, but that never happened. A couple times he told me not to worry about keeping a story in the book, when I was afraid it might be inappropriate. The only time he made suggestions was when I made factual errors on dates or locations. He helped me with this book in the same manner as he coached; he let me make the mistakes, then pointed out the errors without breaking my enthusiasm.

Jack didn't treat players differently; he handled each one of us as separate individuals to get the most out of us. It didn't seem fair sometimes but what became clear is that Jack was a master motivator. If he ever demeaned or berated his players, it was for the sole purpose of motivating them to play better, not out of anger or for his own ego. Jack treated us as adults, a status we rarely deserved. In doing the research for this book, I learned many new things about Jack as a person and coach. He is a truly gifted individual. Jack Barzee is my friend and mentor.

There is another coach that I need to acknowledge and that is my brother Mike Gibbons. Mike was my coach for one year at Bemidji State University. As a young kid I idolized him as a player, and he helped me more than he will ever know. It was his collegiate experience that allowed me to go from being cut in high school to becoming an All-American in college. He recruited me to go to Bemidji State University, after the Dubuque season; but at the last minute, I chose St. Thomas College because they gave me a better financial package. I thought I knew better, but ended up regretting my decision. I left St. Thomas and returned to Bemidji State only to find out my brother was to be the head coach. It was both a blessing and a curse. The season ended with us crying in each other arms after losing the national championship game, a moment I will never forget; but that is another story for another time.

Jack and Mike were the two men that allowed me to be part of the stories written in this book. Without them I would still be just another kid that wasn't quite good enough to make his high school team.

There was one other coach that motivated me but he never coached me. In the summer of 1979, Doug Woog, the Minnesota Gopher hockey coach pulled me aside during a summer league game to inquire what my name was and what high school I played for. When I told him that I didn't play high school hockey because I was cut, he didn't skip a beat. He said "Well, keep playing kid, you're going to be good someday." That was an affirmation that I could play at the same level as any other high school hockey player in Minnesota. I have no idea what motivated Mr. Woog to talk to me, but his words had a lasting effect.

It has been my pleasure and an honor to write these stories for my teammates and *with* my teammates. Several of them said that even though we were all very different people, we got along so well. However, I don't believe that we were that much different. We were all good-natured, strong principled kids who chose not to dwell on the differences but instead on our common goals. There is an unbreakable bond of love with your teammates that develops when you win a championship. There is no greater bond in sports. Inside that locker room, we became brothers.

Many a night was spent on the phone talking with my former Saints teammates, while gathering information for this book. The conversations ended after an hour or so, but the smile I got from talking to each of them lasted for days. It was what kept me going. Most of my teammates claimed to remember nothing from that season. "It was too long ago," they said. But after talking for a short time, they shared stories they thought had been erased. Many times they gave me juicy details about a story that I had long forgotten. All of my "brothers" are still champions, not just on the rink but in life as well.

There are a few teammates that I want to recognize for their individual help with this project. After the last reunion Mark Jasken wrote me an email saying that I had a way with words. That helped me to think that I could actually do a project like this. Jask told me on several occasions that he loved to go back to those days and relive the stories. His kind words helped motivate me immensely.

Inside The Locker Room

While interviewing Reegs I learned that he had written his own book. I immediately ordered his book on Amazon. It is a truly inspiring biography that takes you inside the world of the mentally handicapped and those who care for them. Although Reegs freely admits that he will not win an award for his use of the English language, his story will make you laugh and touch your heart. I strongly recommend "A Ward of the State" by Jeffery Reagan. Sharing his experience helped me tremendously. He very graciously advised me on the pitfalls of an endeavor like this. Reegs is still my captain.

December 1st and 2nd of 2017 were the only two days of the season where I could make the trip to Dubuque to see the current Saints organization. Ironically, Nordsy was scheduled to be in Dubuque on business the same weekend. We went to a Saints game together and went into the early hours of the morning talking, not just about the old days but also about life in general. We fell asleep at about 2 a.m. We woke up at 6 a.m. and picked up right where we left off. Although Nordsy is very busy with his entrepreneurial pursuits, he is always the motivation behind the reunions. The same can be said for this book.

On that same weekend I met up with two other people that felt like teammates. Al Stoltz and Mike Waddick skated in more games than any player. They shared their incredible stories of becoming on-ice officials in a more innocent time in hockey, where a good effort, a good heart and passing a test got you an AHAUS patch, a striped jersey and the right to step out on the ice and face the danger. These two individuals talked openly about their time on the ice and inside their locker room. I hope they get the recognition they deserve for helping the Saints organization get on its feet in those early years. They are extremely good-hearted people, and they trusted me with details, good and bad. Their stories helped to shed light on the blossoming hockey community in Dubuque.

Of course, I have to recognize my old roommate, Worps. Without his insults and bizarre form of leadership, most of the stories in this book would never

have happened. Worps and his wife, Teri, were good sports when they proofed the first few chapters. Surprisingly, they did not mind that I made fun of Worps' personality disorders. I guess they live through it every day, so they consider it normal. Sometimes the truth doesn't hurt.

The current Dubuque Fighting Saints organization was extremely kind and friendly, which is not surprising considering they live in Dubuque. They were gracious to my requests for information and took time to research my requests. I initially reached out to Bill Snook, and he took me under his wing. He made sure my visit to the Mystique Community Ice Center was productive and pleasant. Doc Field was also helpful and accepting of my calls and requests. The Saints have a valuable asset in Doc Field.

Finally, I can't say enough about the people of Dubuque. In 1980, when we first arrived, I knew there was something special about the hockey community in Dubuque. Their kindness and hospitality is second to none. During the season we were served meals at too many family homes to list here. We also made good friends with several families along the way. One example was Gary and Cindy Dolphin. At the end of the season they sent me a personal card that I have to this day...in my scrapbook, somewhere. I distinctly remember thinking that they must have sent those things out like Christmas cards to all the players, but that was not the case. It made me feel special.

Folks like Jim and Ginny Denman adopted the whole team in 1980. Jim calls the former Saints from all the early years his friends and keeps in touch with players from several seasons. He helped motivate me initially with his kindness and hospitality, just like he did with all the guys back in 1980.

During my December trip I planned on getting a hotel room to have some quiet time to write parts of this book. Little did I know I would have to turn down so many offers of a place to stay that it would wear me down. I finally accepted the offer of Chuck and Peggy Haas. I spent that Saturday taking a nap in their living room and later talking with Chuck as he did yard work...in December. Sadly, Peg passed away a few months after my visit. I realized that Peg Haas's brand of hospitality was special. Peg will be missed.

In 1981 the city of Dubuque presented the Key to the City and a plaque as an Honorary Citizen of Dubuque to the players. Some people may say that the two recognitions were symbolic and not really valuable. But I say that those honors are priceless, coming from the people of Dubuque. I proudly display those plaques on my wall today.

I want to close by recognizing my family's help with the writing of this book. If my daughter Maggie had not gone back for her senior year of college soccer, I would not have spent many hours on the road organizing and reliving chapters of this book in my head. I literally drove to places like Minot, ND, with the radio off and my wife either sleeping or working on crafts, while I lost myself in 1980 keeping only a partial focus on the highway. My daughter Kassie, a fulltime art teacher and part-time graphic designer, created the cover and helped with the pictures. My son Cal, a Marketing/Finance professional, shared his practical thoughts. My beautiful wife, Marie, allowed me to spend night after night on the recliner in silence. She told me she did not want to read the book until it was completed. She is wise beyond *my* years.

A special thank you to Joe and Georgia Baxter, Tom Hill, Doug Jass, and all the rest of the hockey community in Dubuque. Your hospitality was appreciated immensely by all the players and will never be forgotten. To all of you who were fans in 1980-81, I want to thank you all on behalf of my teammates.

The 1980-81 season was one of the best times of my life and a great learning experience. Writing this book was like living it all over again.

Gibby,

#5 in your program, #1 in your heart ☺

Gibbons

About Inside The Locker Room:

Inside The Locker Room is a series of books written by Denny Gibbons. This series brings you the real-life stories from the game of hockey. Some are humorous, some are idiotic, some are tragic, but all of them are real events.

Look for these additional books from the *Inside The Locker Room* book series coming in the future:

"Inside The Locker Room: The Undefeated Season": A look inside the 1984 Bemidji State University men's record setting National Championship season. If you think the Saints did a lot of crazy and irrational things...wait until you read the college version!

"Inside The Ref Room": Step inside the referee's locker room and listen to their stories about the game, the angry coaches, the disrespectful players and the unruly fans.

"Inside The Coaches Office": These hockey coaches will entertain you with their true stories of victory and defeat, their quirky type A personalities and their insatiable drive to win.

Keep up to date by following the *Inside The Locker Room* book series on Facebook at:

www.facebook.com/itlrbooks

Made in the USA
Columbia, SC
08 February 2019